The
Hidden Meaning
of
BIRDS

a spiritual field guide

Explore the
Symbology & Significance
*of These Divine
Winged Messengers*

ARIN MURPHY-HISCOCK
Author of *The Green Witch*

ADAMS MEDIA
NEW YORK   LONDON   TORONTO   SYDNEY   NEW DELHI

Adams Media
An Imprint of Simon & Schuster, Inc.
100 Technology Center Drive
Stoughton, MA 02072

First Adams Media trade paperback edition April 2019

ADAMS MEDIA and colophon are trademarks of Simon & Schuster.

For information about special discounts for bulk purchases, please contact Simon & Schuster Special Sales at 1-866-506-1949 or business@simonandschuster.com.

The Simon & Schuster Speakers Bureau can bring authors to your live event. For more information or to book an event contact the Simon & Schuster Speakers Bureau at 1-866-248-3049 or visit our website at www.simonspeakers.com.

Interior design by Erin Alexander
Interior images: Albatross, Blackbird, Bluebird, Cardinal, Chickadee, Cormorant, Crane, Crow, Dove, Duck, Eagle, Egret, Finch, Flamingo, Goldfinch, Goose, Grackle, Gull, Hawk, Heron, Hummingbird, Ibis, Kingfisher, Lark, Loon, Mockingbird, Nuthatch, Oriole, Osprey, Owl, Parakeet, Pelican, Plover, Puffin, Quail, Raven, Robin, Sandpiper, Sparrow, Stork, Swan, Thrush, Turkey, Vulture, Waxwing, Whip-poor-will, Woodpecker, and Yellow Warbler from *120 Audubon Bird Prints* by John James Audubon, New York: Dover Publications, 2008

Blue Jay, Cuckoo, Falcon, Grouse, Magpie, Nighthawk, Petrel, Swallow, and Swift from *Audubon's Birds of America* by Roger Tory Peterson and Virginia Marie Peterson, New York: Abbeville Press Publishers, 1981

Kestrel, Partridge, Starling, and Wren © fineartamerica.com/John James Audubon

Pigeon © Getty Images/Ruskpp

Tree silhouette © Neubau Welt

Manufactured in China

10 9 8 7 6 5

Library of Congress Cataloging-in-Publication Data has been applied for.

ISBN 978-1-5072-1026-0
ISBN 978-1-5072-1027-7 (ebook)

Contains material adapted from the following title published by Adams Media, an Imprint of Simon & Schuster, Inc.: *Birds—A Spiritual Field Guide* by Arin Murphy-Hiscock, copyright © 2012, ISBN 978-1-4405-2688-6.

Table of Contents

Introduction

Birds soar above us, serving as a link between our earthbound lives and the glorious mystery of the beyond. They inspire us to look up, to reach out, to yearn for more. As we look beyond the day-to-day, we strive to accomplish more and to better ourselves in ways we may not otherwise have considered. But birds do more than just speak to our souls. They are creatures of the air, the element that Western culture usually associates with the mind and thus the powers of thought, wisdom, knowledge, and intuition. It's no wonder, then, that for centuries humans from cultures around the world such as Mesopotamia, Sumer, ancient Egypt, China, Japan, Celtic nations, and more have, subconsciously or otherwise, felt drawn to birds and viewed them as messengers or representatives of some kind of mystical communication.

We keep birds as pets, to enjoy their beauty and songs. We keep birds as livestock, to partake of their nourishment. We draw and paint birds, using them as symbols for innumerable virtues. We celebrate their songs in our music. Truly, birds are a magical and omnipresent part of our lives, and because we see them so frequently in our environments, we are drawn to observe them and to make something of their presence.

What does it mean to see a cardinal when you're on your way to the store, or to witness a blue jay eating spiders in your neighbor's back yard? When a hawk soars across the highway, what significance might it have? Read on to learn the history of our winged messengers, how to interpret their signs, and how you can use them to divine the secrets of your own life.

How to Use This Book

The majority of references in this book pertain to wild birds that you are likely to encounter. You'll read about birds that you're more likely to see in the woods, a park, or your own neighborhood; this gives their divinatory meanings immediacy and vitality.

It's important to note that *this is not a scientific field guide*, nor is it designed to be. If you really need to identify a bird, please use a proper field guide such as *Peterson Field Guide to Birds of North America*, *Collins Bird Guide: The Most Complete Guide to the Birds of Britain and Europe*, or other such reference book. You can even get apps for your smartphone to help you identify birds when you're on the go, such as the Audubon Birds regional apps or the Collins Bird Guide app that covers the Western Palearctic region (Europe, North Africa, and parts of the Middle East).

This book focuses on the inspiration, spiritual significance, folklore, symbolism, and divinatory meaning associated with different birds. To help you understand what the bird you've seen is trying to tell you, each bird entry includes the following information:

Name information: This can include the species name, the order and family if necessary to clarify, and/or a common name. Throughout this book, rather than extensive detail about all the different species within a genus, you'll find one overall entry for most birds (for example, the owl) and within that entry, anything specific associated with one particular species (barn owl, great horned owl, etc.) will be addressed. However, there isn't a specific way to determine the spiritual significance of an ornithological subspecies, and it's not going to make a deep impact on the symbolism if the blackbird you see is a European blackbird or an American blackbird.

But what's the difference between all these classifications? They provide different levels of specificity in the taxonomic classification of living creatures and various organisms. There are eight in total, but I refer to four at various times in the entries on each bird, depending on how specific the entry is:

- **Species:** The most specific classification, applied only to one kind of bird within a greater *genus*.
- **Genus:** A group of organisms or creatures that share certain qualities, values, or natural characteristics, within a larger *family*.
- **Family:** A group of related organisms or creatures that share certain qualities, values, or natural characteristics, within a larger *order*.
- **Order:** A group of related organisms or creatures grouped according to how they share certain qualities, values, or natural characteristics. Basically, an order is the most general grouping; the family has a more specific set of things in common; the genus is determined by yet another more specific set of common characteristics; and the species is the most precise way to differentiate an individual kind of bird.

Popular and common variants/subspecies/other names: This list cannot be exhaustive, of course, and will only refer to common subspecies or associated species. You'll find that some subspecies or variants have been pointed out for the sake of interest, but this information doesn't affect the symbolism that you'll take from your encounter.

Geographic distribution: This indicates where the bird can mostly be found worldwide.

Environment: This explains the kind of surroundings or habitat where the bird is most likely to be found.

Physical description: This describes what the bird looks like. Note: the measurements given in this book are rough averages, usually between the male and female of the species.

Interesting facts: Again, this cannot be exhaustive; this is a selection of facts about the bird's call, mating habits, and behavior pertinent to its symbolic meaning.

Myths, folklore, and cultural associations: This is a series of references to the bird's appearances in cultural myths, popular culture, and legend. It's important to understand that a lot of folklore is vague and doesn't necessarily have an identifiable source; like an old wives' tale, something can be part of the general body of lore belonging to a bird and familiar or important to people, and yet not be traceable. If a piece of folklore has an identifiable provenance such as a geographic cultural source, it has been included; otherwise, it is noted as a legend.

Omens and divinatory meaning: This suggests what seeing this bird might mean for you.

Associated energies: This quick reference discusses the energies associated with the bird. Energies encompass the traditional correspondences that have arisen from symbology, mythology, and various cultural perceptions, all combined into a general mélange of traditionally associated correspondences.

Associated seasons: This tells you the season in which the bird is most active, or the season that correlates with its energies. The seasons represent the following:

- **Spring:** New beginnings, sowing, fertility, children, new endeavors
- **Summer:** Fullness, growth, expansion
- **Autumn:** Ripeness, harvest, preparation, resolution
- **Winter:** Death, tranquility, hibernation, rest, introspection

Element associations: This shows which of the four elements—earth, air, fire, or water—the bird is associated with. Generally, this is air, but a bird's color, habitat, or activity may link it with other elements as well. For example, waterfowl also correspond to the element of water. Here is a brief reference to the energies associated with the elements according to Western tradition. You will notice that some concepts appear more than once, and with different elements. This is not unusual, nor is it an error; some qualities cross over between certain elements.

- **Air:** Intellect, knowledge, wisdom, information, freedom, communication
- **Fire:** Inspiration, creativity, passion, vitality, purification
- **Water:** Dreams, intuition, transformation, purification, emotion
- **Earth:** Stability, plenty, abundance, nourishment, grounding

Color associations: This explains the meanings connected with the bird's primary colors. Colors are thought to have a specific energy vibration to them, each with a different effect, influence, or association. Here is a rough guide to Western tradition's color associations:

- **Black:** Encompasses all, grounding, richness, fertility
- **Brown:** Nurturing, grounding, comfort, hearth and home
- **Red:** Vitality, activity, cheer, passion, courage
- **Blue:** Healing, happiness, tranquility, truth
- **Green:** Health, abundance, growth
- **Yellow/Gold:** Joy, clarity, wealth, abundance, solar energy
- **Orange:** Vitality, creativity, enthusiasm
- **Purple:** Spirituality, richness, command, respect
- **Gray/Silver:** Wisdom, neutrality, illusion, lunar energy, peace
- **White:** Purity, peace, purification, blessing, innocence

If other bird entries might supplement the information in the entry you're consulting, I'll point them out. For example, if you've seen an egret, reading about heron and stork symbolism can help you understand more, as the species are closely related and these birds are often mistaken for one another.

Keep a Journal

Although you should use this book for reference, if you're going to examine birds seriously as a form of divination it makes sense to keep track of what kinds of birds you see and what their messages mean to you. Keeping a record of the birds you see allows you to return to your notes and realize the connections between the events in your life and your bird sightings. You can use your current journal, if you keep one, or begin a new one dedicated to the purpose. This allows you to use the information found here to figure out what your bird observations really mean for you and your life.

In order to get the most out of journaling your experiences, you'll want to consider many points as you take notes. The key things to pay attention to include:

- The date and time.
- The location.
- The weather.
- The moon phase.
- The kind of bird that brought you the message/had a message for you.
- What you were doing/thinking/feeling when you saw the bird.
- How you were feeling *before* you saw the bird.
- The immediate emotions the sighting evoked and your first impressions about what the bird's message might be.
- The thoughts that came to mind about the sighting. Were you reminded of someone special or of an event in your past?
- What you were thinking or feeling *after* the encounter. Did the bird have any effect on your mood or mental state?
- The situations in your life that might be connected to or affected by the bird's message.
- The way the bird's message resonates with you (this may be sketchy when you begin, but you'll gradually build up a body

of personal lore; for example, crows may always mean you forgot your keys).

Leave room to go back later to review an entry. Be sure to make later notes about how the sighting impacted you and how hindsight helped you see how the message was valuable. Remember, keeping records is essential to constructing a meaningful relationship with a living, responsive, nature-based system of divination. The more you're able to see the connections between your life and the messages the birds are trying to convey, the more you'll understand about yourself. So read on to learn more about the beautiful mysteries of our feathered friends.

PART I

The Mystery of Birds

Birds are so omnipresent, it's no wonder that superstition and a body of lore have grown up around them. Before we begin to look at the specific lore associated with particular birds in each individual entry, it's important to realize that there are many ways to involve them as augurs or divinatory partners in your life. Part I of this book explores the history of bird divination and gives details on how you can develop a personal method of interpretation unique to you and your experiences.

Chapter 1

Historical Bird Divination

In many cultures throughout history, birds have been seen as symbols of divine inspiration—a supernatural link between the gods and humankind—because of their connection to the sky and their freedom to travel between earth and heaven. Birds are so fascinating to humankind that their behavior has inspired countless forms of divination.

In general, *augury* is the term used for divination made by observing the flight of birds. Although it has since been used to cover just about any kind of soothsaying or fortune-telling, augury refers more specifically to observing the natural behavior of animals or birds. In bird-specific augury, the sky was divided into sections; how birds flew from one section to another indicated what was to come or signified something specific according to the culture. For example, if a bird wheeled left, it might mean one thing; if it flew from the southeast corner of the sky to the northwest it might mean another. *Ornithoscopy* or *ornithomancy* is the study of omens associated with birds, particularly birds in flight. *Alectryomancy* was divination made by observing a bird (usually a chicken) as it fed on grain scattered around a circle of letters, or by reciting the alphabet and noting at which letters the bird moved or called out. And *haruspication*, a well-known method of divination practiced by inspecting the entrails of a sacrificed animal, also employed birds. Eggs were used in divination as well, with *oomancy* or *ovomancy* being the interpretation of the shapes of egg whites as they drift through water.

These different types of divination have been used through history, with differing cultural emphasis and importance. Various countries and cultures perceived birds as carrying different messages. In China, the calls of black birds, particularly ravens, were considered powerful omens examined in relation to the time of day when they were heard and the direction from which the sound came. Birdsong heard at various times can mean different things for other cultures as well.

Unfortunately, ancient cultures rarely recorded their systems of divination. Interpreting omens was often the province of the priesthood or tribal shaman, and if records were made, they either have not survived or were not thought important enough to preserve. Additionally, consider that the interpretation of omens wasn't necessarily codified; it could be very subjective depending on the situation for which the divination was being done. This is an important lesson: bird divination is a very fluid system that can differ greatly from person to person (or culture to culture, or situation to situation) and thus cannot necessarily have a concrete list of what a specific appearance, motion, or call means.

All this is, in fact, an encouraging thing. It's a precedent that allows you the freedom to construct your own interpretation of bird sightings and encounters, as outlined in Chapter 2.

Modern Bird Divination

Looking to birds for spiritual guidance can be a fascinating and enriching pursuit. It can be incredibly easy and yet incredibly frustrating in its vagueness. But with modern bird divination, it's important to realize that the onus of deciphering meaning falls on your shoulders; it's up to you to create your own context for your interpretation.

Much of your interpretation will be, like birds themselves, freeform and boundless. There's a lot of intuitive input in a system like this. What a robin means to you one day may not necessarily be what it means to you the next day, and that's fine. In fact, that's good. A personal divination system should be flexible enough to incorporate new information and observation, as well as taking into account your intuition on a daily basis. If you think a crow is telling you to turn back and double-check to make sure your front door is locked, then that's what it's telling you, even if you'll never find that particular divinatory meaning attached to a crow in any book or historical augury system. And a crow may never tell you to check the lock on your front door again. Part of the key to working successfully with birds as divinatory creatures is being open to their messages, especially on an individual basis.

When trying to divine meaning from a bird's symbology take the following ideas into consideration.

Knowledge Is Power

When you see a bird, find out as much as you can about it. What kind of environment does it usually live in? Is it a bird of prey or a songbird? Don't read too much into predator/prey classifications—a bird of prey is not necessarily better than the bird it preys upon. However, it can be instructive to look up information on the birds a predator hunts to round out your understanding of the message being given to you. If the bird you see is connected to another bird in some way, perhaps by threatening its habitat or food supply, look into that bird as well. You can often get a secondary message that way.

Listen Up

In general, this book uses language that assumes you're seeing the bird. There are many ways of observing something, however. Birds, in particular, can be tricky. You might see a bird, but then again, you might hear it. Birds such as thrushes and whip-poor-wills are more often heard than seen. We don't have room or the ability here to go into what each bird's calls sound like, but you are encouraged to look them up online. The Cornell Lab of Ornithology (www.allaboutbirds.org) at Cornell University in Ithaca, New York, has a decent database of birdcalls; just look up the bird name and follow the tabs on the bird's information page. It can be hard to track down a bird by its call alone, but if you familiarize yourself with the calls of birds common to your region, you'll arm yourself with knowledge you can use to identify the birds later. You can also download smartphone apps to help you identify birdcalls.

Location

Where you live will naturally influence the kinds of birds you see regularly. Here's a rough list of the types of common birds you can find in various environments. Note that these lists are not exhaustive; they don't include every bird in the book associated with that kind of environment. Nor are these lists universally applicable to every city, swamp, or forest.

Cities and Suburbs

- Blackbird
- Blue jay
- Cardinal
- Chickadee
- Crow
- Dove
- Gull
- Hawk
- Pigeon
- Robin
- Sparrow
- Starling

Forested Areas

- Blue jay
- Cardinal
- Chickadee
- Crow
- Nuthatch
- Owl
- Robin
- Thrush

Wetlands, Shores, and Swampy Areas

- Blackbird
- Duck
- Goose
- Gull
- Loon
- Pelican
- Swan

Farmlands, Prairies, and Fields

- Blackbird
- Crow
- Dove
- Hawk
- Jay
- Owl
- Partridge
- Pigeon
- Robin
- Sparrow
- Starling

Mountainous Areas

- Eagle
- Falcon
- Hawk

Use common sense too. If you're on a homestead and raise ducks, seeing one is not going to carry the same weight that seeing a duck might if you live in the city and don't encounter them on a daily basis. Also, what the duck means to you will be different. It may represent home, hearth, daily life, or chores, whereas to a city dweller it might be a reminder of rural, pastoral life and the idyllic associations those things can have.

A final word concerning bird identification: Does it matter if you can identify the bird you saw as a mountain bluebird or an indigo bunting? Perhaps; perhaps not. Don't stress yourself trying to make sure you actually have the correct identification for the bird you've seen. Your location will always be the first clue (for example, the robin seen in North America is a thrush, while the European robin is a member of the flycatcher family, and if you're in Australia you may know the tomtit, or the Australian robin, which is a member of a third family altogether), but it's also important to take your sighting in the spirit it's been offered. If you think you've seen a bluebird (and really, why would you think it might be a robin-type from a different family if your location wouldn't feature that different bird with a red breast?), then follow your intuition and read up on the general robin entry. That may be exactly what your subconscious wants you to do.

Alternatively, what if you can't figure out if what you saw was a small raven or a really big crow? If you're not familiar with the differences, read about them both. They're both corvids (the family that contains crows, ravens, and jays, among others), and much of their lore overlaps.

You can see how fluid and how vague this system can be. So much of it depends on you. Interpreting natural omens is a very personal thing, and it rarely gives you a detailed answer. However, you can consciously work with birds through meditation and other exercises to try to hone in on a particular bird's symbolism and energy.

Chapter 3

Working with Birds Spiritually

There are many different ways to work with birds from a spiritual viewpoint. And in fact, you can work with birds beyond just observing them in their natural environments or coming across their images in films or books. Here you'll learn how to consciously work with the powers and concepts represented by each bird by connecting to the bird's energies through meditation or other methods.

Look for Freeform Guidance

If you're looking for personal direction from a winged messenger, try this freeform technique. You can find guidance quickly by going outside to a park or a garden and sitting quietly. Wait for the first bird to appear. Instead of noting what kind of bird it is and reading about its associations, look at the following things:

- What direction did it come from?
- How many birds are there?
- What kind of movements are they making?
- Do they stay in the air, or do they land?
- If they fly past, how high do they fly?
- If they land, what activity do they engage in?

The most basic of these is noting whether the first bird you see appears on your left or right. Traditional Western association with left and right suggests that if a bird appears on your left, the answer to your question is either no or the outcome is negative; if a bird appears on your right, the answer is yes or the outcome is positive. If you are left-handed, or have a special preference for the left, you might want to flip these associations. Another way of approaching this kind of quick divination is to associate the left with the past, suggesting that the root of the problem or clues to its solution lie in the past. The right indicates that an issue associated with the future is affecting the situation.

If the bird appears directly in front of you, this could be the universe's way of saying "maybe" or "try again later." Or, it might mean that the answer is right in front of you and you only have to allow yourself to see it. If the bird appears behind you (you might have to rely on sound for that identification), it might indicate that things aren't ready to be revealed yet. General folklore suggests that if the bird flies away from you, the augury is unfavorable; if it flies toward you, the augury is favorable.

Employ Bird Energy As Spiritual Guidance

Apart from actually seeing or hearing a physical example of a bird in real life, how can you work with birds as symbols or omens if you come across the mention of one in a book or article, or see one in a film or on television? What if you want to seek guidance from the bird kingdom but can't go outside?

If you are in need of guidance from a particular bird, or if you wish to work with a bird's energy for a period of time but don't know which one to choose, you can do one of several things:

- Flip through this book with your eyes closed and choose a page at random.
- Use an existing commercially available set of oracle cards, such as G.G. Carbone's very pretty *Bird Signs* set designed in collaboration with Mary Ruzicka; shuffle through them and choose one card at random.
- Take a set of index cards and write the names of birds on them, or find pictures of the birds and glue them on the cards. Write keywords below the picture if you like. Consult this book or others for an associated message, or start making notes in your own journal about what the bird means in general and in specific to you, and refer to it when you draw a card from your own deck.

Alternatively, if you want to call a bird to you without knowing which one to work with, you can use the Find a Bird Guide meditation later in this chapter.

Totems and Spirit Guides

A totem or spirit guide is an entity that guides or protects you. Some people use them as identifiers of various parts of their personalities. Traditionally, a spirit guide was an entity that shamans worked with.

This entity served as a go-between or companion on the shaman's journeys to the spirit world to bring back information that would help or guide the shaman's tribe or clan. Spirit guides are generally not chosen; they are either assigned to the shaman when she or he is initiated into the mysteries of the Otherworld, usually by otherworldly forces, or the spirit guide chooses the shaman.

A totem is an animal, plant, or entity that serves as an emblem or identifying symbol for a clan, tribe, or other family group, or for a specific individual. For example, the North American Cherokee nation consists of seven clans, some of which are identified by animal totems such as Deer, Wolf, and Bird. A totem is sometimes considered a tribal ancestor of sorts. It is given honor and great significance, and there are often taboos surrounding the killing or eating of the totem animal.

In contemporary parlance, we often talk about voluntarily working with totems or the energy of a specific bird or animal. In a way, looking to birds as a kind of divinatory system is a form of perceiving them as temporary spirit guides. In this instance, we are seeing them as messengers from the Otherworld, from the Divine, or from the universe at large.

Working with a Specific Bird

You may already have a specific bird that is a personal symbol or totem. Is there a bird that you have been drawn to for most of your life or a bird that has popped up repeatedly? Do people give you images or art featuring a particular bird, even if you don't consciously display a liking for it? This bird may be a personal totem, representing and reflecting part of your spirit. Read about the bird; explore its symbolism; research mythology and cultural folklore beyond what is presented in this book. Thank the bird for being a part of your life by formally welcoming it, with either a poem or other artwork or simply a heartfelt spoken thanks.

On a very basic level, you can mentally visualize the bird you've chosen. You could carry a photograph or postcard of it, or draw your own picture. You might find a piece of jewelry with the bird's image on it or a piece of art featuring the bird to display in your home. Educate yourself about the bird's habits, its habitat, and its lifestyle. Read about conservation efforts, and if you have the resources, engage in helping to spread the word or donate to a reputable charity that works with that particular bird.

If you do choose to work with a specific bird for a period of time to get to know it better or because you think its energies could strengthen yours in a time of need, then you can consciously call that bird to you by practicing the following meditation.

Meditation: Align with a Specific Bird

Find a quiet place where you will not be disturbed. You may wish to prepare the area by burning a purifying incense such as sandalwood, frankincense, or cedar. If you are familiar with smudging, the practice of cleansing the energy of an area with sage smoke, then you may choose to do this. You may wish to play quiet music or a recording of birdsong or nature sounds. Keep the volume low.

Sit down and close your eyes. Make sure your clothing is unrestrictive and you are sitting comfortably. Take a few deep breaths, exhaling softly after each one. Feel your muscles release any tension they may be holding, starting at your feet and moving up through your body. Clear your mind. Your goal is to be in a relaxed state, undistracted by your surroundings.

When you feel ready, in your mind's eye see a landscape. Depending on your preference it may be a meadow, a forest, a beach, or a cliff. Allow a request to form in your heart, and the image of the bird upon which you are focusing to form in your mind. Make the mental image as detailed and precise as possible. Reach out with your feelings or mind for the bird you have chosen to meet and ask the bird to come to you. Speak aloud to call it, if you so desire, or imagine yourself speaking in this landscape.

Visualize the bird coming to you. It may circle around you; land on the ground near you; or land on your hand, shoulder, or head. Welcome it; thank it for coming and for agreeing to work with you for however long you require, or until it decides that you have learned all that you can learn from it and it leaves.

Tell the bird why you have chosen to work with it. You may want to talk about its energies or traditional associations, and your needs or the weaknesses you would like to bolster. The bird may communicate with you in some fashion: it may speak to you, it may communicate silently mind to mind, or you may receive impressions of ideas or emotions from it. Be open to receiving any and all communication from the bird. Remember, you have chosen to work with this bird for a specific reason; you may not like what it has to say, but the encounter is for your benefit.

When you feel ready (or when the bird decides this session is over) thank the bird again for agreeing to work with you and bid it farewell for now. Allow the landscape and environment that you have visualized to fade away, and gradually become aware of your body again. Slowly take deep breaths to reawaken your physical self and wiggle your fingers and toes gently, then move your arms and legs carefully.

Write about your experience in either a daily journal or meditation journal if you already keep one, or start a journal devoted to working with birds. Make an initial record of what you instinctively feel the bird represents to you, then look up its traditional associations. Building up a record like this allows you to assemble a reference balanced between what tradition or the general perception of the bird says it means and your own intuitive connections. This reference will help you deepen your understanding of the bird and its meaning to you. ∼

Let a Guide Come to You

Sometimes you need a guide to address issues that you aren't consciously aware of. If you are open to the idea of working with a bird that chooses you instead, that bird will be the right one for you at this moment in time. Use the following meditation to call a guide to you.

Meditation: Find a Bird Guide

Find a quiet place where you will not be disturbed. You may wish to prepare the area by burning a purifying incense such as sandalwood, frankincense, or cedar. If you are familiar with smudging, the practice of cleansing the energy of an area with sage smoke, then you may choose to do this. You may wish to play quiet music or a recording of birdsong or nature sounds. Keep the volume low.

Sit down and close your eyes. Make sure your clothing is unrestrictive and you are sitting comfortably. Take a few deep breaths, exhaling softly after each one. Feel your muscles release any tension they may be holding, starting at your feet and moving up through your body. Clear your mind. Your goal is to be in a relaxed state, undistracted by your surroundings.

When you feel ready, envision a landscape in your mind's eye. It may be a meadow, a forest, a beach, or a cliff. Just allow a landscape to form in your mind's eye. Don't consciously direct it; allow it to form on its own.

Allow a request to form in your heart. Reach out for a bird to come to you, a bird whose energies will support yours and bring you the strength and energies you need in your life right now. Speak aloud, if you desire, or imagine yourself speaking in this landscape.

Wait for a response. You may hear a particular song or call, or you may see a bird as it joins you in the visualized landscape. Don't be disappointed if nothing appears immediately. Repeat your wordless appeal for a guide or your spoken invitation for a guide to join you. If a bird does not appear, end your meditation journey and try again another day. Over the next few days, be on the alert—the bird may appear to you in some form in daily life, so watch for feathered messengers crossing your path, or for birds appearing in films or books.

If a bird does appear in your meditation, welcome it. Absorb what details you can about the bird that has replied to your appeal. You may be able to identify the bird right away, or you may not recognize it at all. Take a good look at its size, shape, and the color of its plumage, and listen to its call. If it flies, note the silhouette it makes against the sky; this might help you identify it later. Don't be discouraged if it doesn't hold still long enough for you to get a really close look at it.

The bird will be welcoming and willing to be with you, or it wouldn't have appeared. Talk to it; thank it for coming and for agreeing to work with you until it judges that you no longer need its support. The bird may communicate with you in some fashion: It may speak to you, it may communicate silently mind to mind, or you may receive impressions of ideas or emotions from it.

Be open to receiving any and all communication from the bird. Don't expect a certain message based on what type of bird it is or limit yourself by listening for something specific. Clear your mind, and be open to the bird's love and energy. Know, too, that the bird's message may be positive or negative, and don't judge the bird based on the content of its message.

When you feel ready (or when the bird decides this session is over) thank the bird again for agreeing to work with you and bid it farewell for now. Allow the landscape and environment that you have visualized to fade away and gradually become aware of your body again. Slowly take deep breaths to reawaken your physical self and wiggle your fingers and toes gently; follow this by carefully moving your arms and legs.

Write about your experience in either a daily journal or meditation journal if you already keep one, or start a journal devoted to working with birds. Make an initial record of what you instinctively feel the bird represents to you, then look up its traditional associations to learn as much as you can from your own observations, feelings, and the available existing lore concerning the bird in question. ∼

The Birds of the Air

Air is the element most frequently associated with birds, and for good reason: most birds fly in some way, shape, or form. Only a few are completely limited to land or water. Here you'll find a meditation to attune yourself to the element of air, so as to deepen your understanding of it. If the birds you wish to work with are earth- or water-based, you can tweak the meditation to reflect their elemental affinity. Instead of flying, imagine yourself settling on the surface of the water, into the leaves of a forest floor, or whatever your chosen bird might do in the environment it prefers. (Working with a bird from a snowy habitat? Use a water meditation as a basis, but think cold.)

It must be emphasized that this meditation is not dependent on the laws of physics. It is imagination, pure and simple. It is meant to help you explore the energy of the element of air and how it pertains to birds.

Meditation: Attune to Air

Find a quiet place where you will not be disturbed. If possible, you may wish to sit outside or by an open window in order to feel the flow of air around you. Failing that, you might consider having a fan on hand, of any material, with which to fan yourself gently at some time during the meditation.

You may wish to prepare the area by burning a purifying incense such as sandalwood, frankincense, or cedar. If you are familiar with smudging, the practice of cleansing the energy of an area with sage smoke, then you may choose to do this. You may also wish to play quiet music or a recording of birdsong or nature sounds, but keep the volume low.

Sit down and close your eyes. Make sure you are wearing unrestrictive clothing and are sitting comfortably. Take a few deep breaths, exhaling softly after each one. Feel your muscles release any tension they may be holding, starting at your feet and moving up through your body. Clear your mind. Your goal is to be in a relaxed state, undistracted by your surroundings.

When you feel ready, visualize a landscape in your mind's eye. Depending on your preference it may be a meadow, a forest, a beach, or a cliff. Envision yourself standing in this landscape. Now, close your eyes in your visualization as you have them closed in real life.

Feel yourself standing in this landscape. Feel the sun on your body, the wind on your skin. With your eyes still closed, note any sounds around you. Is the wind rustling through the leaves on the trees? Do you hear the sound of surf, of waves on a beach? Can you hear birds calling somewhere, or other animals? What scents do you smell? If you open your mouth, does the air have a taste to it? All these things are connected with the element of air. Take time to explore your environment with your senses other than vision.

When you have explored your environment with your senses, take a few more deep, relaxing breaths. Visualize your arms lifting slightly away from your body. Feel the air stirring around your torso, moving your clothing. How does it move your hair?

At this point, if you feel comfortable doing so, visualize yourself shapeshifting easily into a bird of your choice. (For this meditation, choose a flying bird as opposed to one limited to land or water. It doesn't have to be a specific bird; it can be a generic one, so don't get bogged down in detail.) Now feel how the air flows through and around your feathers, how it feels against your legs.

When you feel comfortable, open your wings fully and allow the wind to flow under them. Feel the lift, and begin to flap your wings. Launch yourself into the air, feeling your strong wing beats working with the air and wind to lift yourself higher and higher. Imagine how it feels to soar, to glide, to dip and dive and play in the air. Experiment with how the air presses against various parts of your wings and body; move your tail and discover how it affects your trajectory through the air.

When you are ready, glide back down to earth. Allow the wind to release you, to slide away from where it has wrapped your body. Take a few deep, relaxing breaths, and then visualize yourself returning to your human form. Thank the air and the wind for your experience.

Take a few more breaths, then slowly open your eyes and see the physical environment around you. Wiggle your fingers and toes, then gently move or flex your arms and legs to help you return fully to the real world. Stretch your neck gently, tilting your head from side to side.

Write about your experience in either a daily journal or meditation journal if you already keep one, or start a journal devoted to working with birds. How did you feel at each stage of the experience? Write down details about the sounds, the smells, the sensation of the air. Write about how it felt to fly, what differences you felt when interacting with the element of air as a human and as a bird, and whatever other important observations or feelings you experienced to learn as much as you can from your own observations, feelings, and the available existing lore concerning the bird in question. ⌒

Honor Your Guide

However you choose to begin your spiritual relationship with a bird, it is good manners to honor your guide regularly. You can do so by producing or displaying art featuring the bird, by wearing jewelry inspired by it, or by leaving offerings for it. If your guide is a native local bird, you can probably leave a food offering suited to its diet, but if you end up working with a bird whose habitat is thousands of miles away from yours, feel free to leave symbolic offerings for it in a place set apart for that purpose, such as a home shrine or altar. Honoring it by leaving an offering for the local birds will do, but this should be a last resort. (Be sure to research the dietary requirements of your local feathered friends and also your municipal bylaws on the feeding of wild animals.) You can also donate to a charity or ongoing conservation effort as an offering to the bird spirit with which you are working. Look up local bird sanctuaries or biodomes too; they always need financial support or perhaps volunteers.

As you can see, birds can be a rich spiritual resource, both as guides and inspiration. Constructing your own relationship with such a beautiful, omnipresent aspect of the natural world is a rewarding undertaking, one that can enhance your own connection to the world around you as well as allowing you a glimpse into your own soul. So without further ado, let's take a look at some of the most commonly encountered birds and what messages they can bring us.

PART II

The Birds

In this part you'll find information on the most common birds, along with pictures of each bird for quick identification. As you begin to learn more about these winged messengers, keep in mind that your own experience and intuition are just as valuable as these more traditional references. Don't hesitate to trust your instincts and assign your own, more personal associations to your feathered friends.

Time of Day

While reading about these birds, note that the time of day at which you see each bird will also affect the meaning of the sighting in the following ways:

- **Dawn:** New beginnings, potential
- **Morning:** Expansion
- **Midday:** Balance, power
- **Afternoon:** Reduction, combining
- **Sunset:** Resolution
- **Midnight:** Introspection, power

Keep track of this information as you decipher the symbology behind each sighting.

Albatross

Genus: *Diomedea* (great albatross), *Phoebastria* (North Pacific albatrosses)

Popular and common variants/subspecies/other names: Short-tailed albatross, black-footed albatross

Geographic distribution: Most albatrosses are found in the Southern Hemisphere, with the exception of albatrosses of the North Pacific, which are found off the west coast of North America.

Environment: The albatross is found in coastal areas.

Physical description: The albatross has a long, straight bill with a hook on the end with two tubes along it, one on each side, to allow the bird to expel seawater taken in with food. Its plumage ranges from browns to whites. The black-footed albatross measures approximately 27 inches long, has a wingspan of approximately 80 inches, and weighs about 7 to 9 pounds.

Interesting facts: Albatrosses have an excellent sense of smell. Unlike most waterfowl, they walk very capably on land. When flying, they use a gliding technique that lets them travel much farther forward than they drop on a vertical axis, allowing them to cover a large distance with minimal loss of altitude. Albatrosses are colonial, meaning they live in breeding colonies, generally the one they were born in, and pair bonds usually last for life.

Myths, folklore, and cultural associations: Early on, albatrosses were considered to be guides or incarnations of wandering souls lost at sea, which is why it was considered unlucky to shoot or eat one. They were also used as weather indicators, usually meaning that stormy weather was imminent. However, the albatross became associated with sin, guilt, and punishment with the publication of Samuel Taylor Coleridge's *The Rime of the Ancient Mariner*. In this tale, the albatross is a symbol of guilt and burden, worn about the neck of the sailor who shot it down; thus the bird became seen as the initiator of a series of bad luck.

Omens and divinatory meaning: Albatrosses spend a lot of time gliding, rarely needing to flap their wings. This suggests an efficient use of the resources available to them. If you see an albatross, ask yourself if you're deploying your energy to the best uses. Albatrosses use air currents to propel themselves: look at your life to see what energies you can borrow to help you along and conserve your own energy.

An albatross can also tell you to stay aloft. These birds can spend weeks on end in the air, never fully landing or returning to shore. Keep flying; trust yourself to soar. Don't constantly rush back home to feel safe. Be strong, and strike out on your own.

The albatross's strong connection to its family breeding grounds may inspire you to check in with your family. If you've never done so, take a look at your family history or your cultural traditions. What country or countries do your ancestors come from? What can you learn from their customs and heritage? Learning these kinds of things can enrich who you are and your sense of self.

> **Associated energies:** Conservation of energy, trust in yourself, family, heritage
>
> **Associated seasons:** Fall, winter
>
> **Element associations:** Air, water
>
> **Color associations:** Gray, black, beige, white

Blackbird

Name: Red-winged blackbird

Species: *Agelaius phoeniceus*

Popular and common variants/subspecies/other names: Common blackbird (or Eurasian blackbird, *Turdus merula*)

Geographic distribution: The Eurasian blackbird is found throughout Europe, the UK, Australia, and New Zealand. The red-winged blackbird is found from North through Central America.

Environment: Red-winged blackbirds like being near water, such as swamps, marshes, and waterways, and in residential areas such as suburban locations.

Physical description: The male red-winged blackbird has mainly black plumage with a scarlet shoulder underlined by yellow, and a black beak, whereas the female is dark brown. The average red-winged blackbird measures about 8 inches long, has a wingspan of approximately 14 inches, and weighs about 2 ounces. The Eurasian blackbird is all black, with a yellow bill.

Interesting facts: The Old World blackbirds are members of the thrush family; American blackbirds are birds of the New World Icterid family. They are very territorial.

Myths, folklore, and cultural associations: In medieval religious belief, the blackbird represented desire, particularly physical desire.

Like crows and ravens, the blackbird's dark plumage associated it with nighttime and hidden mysteries. It is also associated with travel between the worlds and shamanic journeys.

The famous nursery rhyme that tells us of "four and twenty blackbirds baked in a pie" is likely based on the dinner entertainment of placing live birds within a pre-baked pie shell that was then covered with a baked pastry lid in order to surprise diners when they cut open the pie.

In Druidic lore, the goddess Rhiannon is accompanied by three birds who usually perch in the World Tree and whose song is a magical lullaby that can put the listener to sleep, enabling them to travel to the Otherworld in their dreams; these birds are often said to be blackbirds.

Omens and divinatory meaning: Examine your behavior or chosen path for hidden motives or potential. If other people are asking you to do something, examine those requests for hidden motive as well.

If you see a blackbird, examine your territory, or your sphere of responsibility. Is someone trying to slip his way in? Look at this person's motives, and if they are malicious or sly, take a stand and let him know in no uncertain terms that what's yours is yours, and you'll defend it if necessary. Blackbirds will attack much larger birds if they come too near their territory; don't shy away from making noise at a corporation or someone important if you need to.

Associated energies: Defense, standing up for your rights or beliefs, hidden potential, hidden motives

Associated seasons: Spring, summer, fall

Element associations: Air, water

Color associations: Black, red, yellow

Blue Jay

Species: *Cyanocitta cristata*

Popular and common variants/subspecies/other names: Gray jay or Canada jay (*Perisoreus canadensis*), Steller's jay (*Cyanocitta stelleri*)

Geographic distribution: Native to North America, the blue jay can be found in southern Canada and throughout the United States from the Midwest to the eastern coastal regions. The Steller's jay is found in western North America from Canada down through Central America. Jays also exist in the Old World but have buff to brown plumage; the blue is native to North America.

Environment: The blue jay is mainly found in mixed forest areas, especially forest edges, and residential areas such as towns and cities. The Steller's jay prefers evergreen forests.

Physical description: The blue jay is a medium-sized songbird that weighs about 3 ounces, measures about 10 inches, and has a wingspan of about 15.5 inches. Like all other corvids (members of the Corvidae family that includes birds such as crows and ravens), jays are fiercely intelligent and social birds, with a loud call that ranges from a harsh cry to close mimicry of other birds or sounds. The blue jay features blue plumage on its back, white or pale gray on its front, and a varied patchwork detail of blue, black, and gray on its wings and tail, with a slightly darker mask around the face. It has a jaunty crest of feathers on the top of the head that raises when the bird is alert; the crest is lowered when the jay is relaxed, especially when feeding a brood or dealing with extended family such as flock mates. The Steller's jay is dark blue with a charcoal gray head and lacks the paler belly of the common blue jay.

Interesting facts: The blue jay stuffs food in a throat pouch while gathering, to store it for later. Blue jays often mate for life, and pairs typically remain monogamous. Blue jays particularly like oak trees and have a fondness for acorns. They have a mystifying and seemingly chaotic migratory pattern that does not appear to depend on their region: some migrate north, others migrate south, some do not migrate at all, and some migrate only in alternate years.

Myths, folklore, and cultural associations: The word *jay* may come from Old French *jai*, meaning "gay," a reference to the bird's bright plumage. The Canada or gray jay (*Perisoreus canadensis*) has a reputation for caching and thieving; *perisoriou* means "to pile up."

As the blue jay is a North American bird, it lacks the older religious symbolism of Old World birds. Instead, it is featured in Native American myths and seems to have been an important figure especially to the Chinook, Sioux, and Coast Salish tribes. In one myth, the jay is said to have had a beautiful voice and became overly proud of it. To punish him, the gods caused the jay's voice to change to the harsh, croak call we know today. In other myths, the blue jay is a trickster figure who works with Coyote or Fox.

The blue jay is the provincial bird of eastern Canada's Prince Edward Island. The provincial bird of British Columbia on Canada's west coast is the Steller's jay.

Omens and divinatory meaning: The jay's strong family bond may be directing you to look to your own family situation. Are you directing more energy into nonfamily areas of your life than into your family itself? The jay may also be urging you to trust your immediate and extended family, including your trusted communities, and by extension to be more alert when dealing with people who are not of these closer relationships. Be fearless when defending your family and the communities in which you participate. The jay's strong flock or family ties also point to its loyalty.

The jay's relationship with oak trees may prompt you to look into the oak's meanings. The oak tends to be associated with strength, durability, timelessness, longevity, and protection. Alternatively, the qualities connected with evergreens, the Steller's jay's preferred tree, include fertility and everlasting life.

The blue jay's familiar talkativeness, coupled with its blue feathers (a color associated with the throat chakra, one of several energy centers found throughout the body), may be urging you to look at your own communication habits and skills. Are you talking a lot and saying not much of substance? Are you communicating the essential truths and facts or burying them in a lot of chaff? The color blue is also linked with purity and spirituality; the blue jay may be coaxing you to follow higher ideals and nourish your spirituality.

Finally, the jay may be reminding you to gather and store a bit extra in order to ensure that you have a safety net if times get tough.

Associated energies: Family bonds, social networks, communication, loyalty, fearlessness

Associated seasons: Spring, summer, fall

Element associations: Earth, air

Color associations: Blue, white, gray, black

Bluebird

Genus: *Sialia*

Family: Turdidae

Popular and common variants/subspecies/other names: Western bluebird (*Sialia mexicana*), mountain bluebird (*Sialia currucoides*), eastern bluebird (*Sialia sialis*); the Eurasian blue tit (*Cyanistes caeruleus*) and azure tit (*Cyanistes cyanus*) are likely the bluebirds of European lore

Geographic distribution: Eastern bluebirds are found east of the Rocky Mountains in North America from southern Canada down to the US states bordering the Gulf of Mexico, and from the southwestern

US state of Arizona to Nicaragua. Mountain bluebirds are found from Alaska south through western Canada and the western United States. Western bluebirds are found from Alaska south through the Canadian Prairie provinces and the western/central United States, to central Mexico. Northern birds will migrate to a more southern area of the species' distribution; southern birds are generally permanent residents. The blue tits of Europe are found in temperate and subarctic zones, as well as western Asia; the azure tits are found in western Russia, with an eastern counterpart there as well.

Environment: Bluebirds prefer open woodland, grasslands, rural areas, farmland, and orchards. Bluebirds are comfortable living near houses and people.

Physical description: Mountain bluebirds are all blue with a paler blue/gray stomach; the female is gray with blue tones. The eastern bluebird is blue and red with a white stomach. The western bluebird is colored similarly to the eastern but also has a small patch of brown between its shoulders. Males and females are generally similar in size; females are only slightly duller in color than males. The bluebird measures approximately 6 to 8 inches long and weighs on average about an ounce.

Interesting facts: Nesting pairs of bluebirds return to the same nest site every year. They nest in cavities and will use man-made cavities for nests if natural hollows are not easily found. Males attract females by placing nesting material in cavities or other nest locations, singing, and through physical activity such as flapping their wings. When the female chooses the location and the male who has prepared it, she builds the nest and incubates the eggs. Bluebirds can produce between two and four broods per year (spring and summer, with southern-living birds producing the higher number of broods). Though territorial, bluebirds are gentle, timid birds, and they face aggressive competition for nesting sites from house sparrows and starlings.

Myths, folklore, and cultural associations: The most significant identifier of the bluebird is, of course, its beautiful blue plumage. Traditionally, the color blue has been associated with the sky, health, and peace, but it is also often connected with sorrow. Blue is also perceived as being a spiritual color, used by artists for the clothing worn by the Virgin Mary. This association likely derived from how precious the pigments to mix blue paint were at one time, and so the color was reserved for the holiest or most-loved religious figures in iconography.

Two popular stories are associated with the bluebird. The first is *L'Oiseau bleu* (literally, *The Blue Bird*) by Madame d'Aulnoy, written in the seventeenth century. In this tale, King Charming is transformed into a bluebird and in this shape supports his beloved Princess Fiordelisa through various challenges. In the early twentieth century, French playwright Maurice Maeterlinck wrote a stage play, also called *L'Oiseau bleu* (known as *The Bluebird of Happiness*), the story of two young children who seek the Bluebird of Happiness in the hopes that it will make their lives better. The children return home empty-handed only to discover their pet bird has all along been the bluebird they sought.

The Native American Navajo people honor the bluebird as associated with the sunrise, and they sing a bluebird song to greet the dawn that translates roughly as "The bluebird speaks to me, 'Get up, grandchild; it is dawn,' it speaks to me." This song is still performed, both recreationally and as a key part of the nine-day winter Nightway ceremony; the song brings the ceremony to completion just before the sun rises on the final day. There is also a Cochiti tribal myth that holds that the bluebird is the firstborn male child of the sun. In Russian lore, the bluebird is an omen of hope.

The mountain bluebird is also the official bird of the US states of Idaho and Nevada.

Omens and divinatory meaning: The bluebird speaks to you of inner calm, peace, balance and harmony, and a genuine love of the self.

Cardinal

Species: *Cardinalis cardinalis*

Popular and common variants/subspecies/other names:
Northern cardinal, Virginia cardinal (now out of use), redbird,
common cardinal

Geographic distribution: The cardinal can be found in southern
parts of eastern Canada and down through the eastern United States
from Maine to Texas. Its range also extends west and south through
Mexico to Guatemala and Belize.

Environment: The cardinal prefers woodland, residential areas, and
swampland.

Physical description: The northern cardinal is a mid-sized songbird with a distinctive crest on the head. The cardinal measures approximately 8.5 inches long, weighs approximately 1.5 ounces, and has a wingspan of about 11 inches. The male is slightly larger than the female and is a vibrant red with a black mask on his face that covers his eyes and throat below the red beak. The female's plumage is a dull red-brown and she has a gray mask.

Interesting facts: The cardinal is a territorial bird that outlines and defends its territory with song. Cardinals mate for life and prefer to remain in the same general area to raise their broods year after year.

Myths, folklore, and cultural associations: The cardinal is easy to spot due to its coloring. It is one of the most popular birds and easily identified by birdwatchers and non-birdwatchers alike.

Like the robin, whose plumage also features a distinctive red patch, the cardinal is often associated with Christmas and the winter season.

The cardinal's name is derived from the high-ranking clerics of the Catholic Church who wear rich red robes. The term *cardinal* is used to denote something with primary or essential qualities, such as a cardinal direction. The word comes from the Latin *cardo*, meaning "hinge."

The Native American Cherokee believe that the cardinal is the daughter of the sun. Legend has it that if you see a cardinal flying upward, toward the sun, you will have good luck. Conversely, if you see it flying down toward the earth, watch out for bad luck.

The cardinal was the first bird to be given state recognition in the United States: in 1926, it was made the state bird of Kentucky. It's also the bird of six other US states (Illinois, Indiana, North Carolina, Ohio, Virginia, and West Virginia), making it the most popular state bird. It is also the name of the St. Louis (Missouri) professional baseball team and the Arizona Cardinals professional football team, and is the mascot of numerous university athletic teams, including the Louisville (Kentucky) Cardinals and the Wesleyan (Connecticut) Cardinals.

Omens and divinatory meaning: Examine the areas of your life in which you are, or should be, a leader. Is your confidence shaky? The cardinal tells you that you can handle it and to believe in yourself.

It is important to be proud of yourself for your abilities or for the things you have achieved. The cardinal's bright red feathers and cheerful song call attention to it wherever it goes. If you see a cardinal, it may be telling you to stand up, lift your head high, and take pride in yourself. Accept compliments that come your way and acknowledge your achievements.

The cardinal's bright red plumage also calls you to open yourself to creative energy. Have you been feeling blocked or dull lately? Are you looking for a new way to express yourself? Call on the cardinal to help you open up and get your creativity flowing again. The red feathers link it with fire, the element of activity, vitality, and passion. If you are feeling lethargic, the cardinal may lend you its energy to help you get back on your feet. Likewise, it can be a good bird with whom to work if you are struggling to handle depression.

If you are having difficulty dealing with anger, however, seeing a cardinal may remind you to take a step or two back. Red is the color of the root chakra, the energy center associated with stability, survival, and security, and feeling unsettled in any of these areas may be influencing your anger issue. Examine the areas of your life connected to these subjects for clues to the source of your emotional state and move to make them better.

Associated energies: Leadership, self-worth, confidence, creativity, vitality, activity

Associated season: Winter

Element associations: Air, fire

Color associations: Red, black

Chickadee

Name: Black-capped chickadee

Species: *Poecile atricapillus* or *Parus atricapillus*

Popular and common variants/subspecies/other names:
Carolina chickadee, mountain chickadee; the European equivalent is
the willow tit

Geographic distribution: The chickadee is found in Canada and
the northern half of the United States. The willow tit is found in most
of northern Europe.

Environment: Chickadees gravitate to treed areas, such as forests or
woodlots, and live well in residential areas. They can also be found in
swamps or marshes.

Physical description: The black-capped chickadee is a popular and easily recognized bird, with a black cap on the top of the head, a short dark bill, a black bib-like patch on the throat and upper chest, and white sides to the face that sweep back over the shoulders. The chest and stomach areas are white, shading into buff or darker brown on the sides. The back, short wings, and long tail are shades of gray. The chickadee measures approximately 5 inches long, with a wingspan of 7 inches and a weight of half an ounce. The overall silhouette suggests a compact, chubby bird.

Interesting facts: Chickadees do not formally migrate but may range southward in their region. These tiny birds can lower their body temperature significantly on cool nights in order to conserve body energy. Chickadees sing out when there is danger or when they find food to call other chickadees to the area, an action that also signals the important information to other small birds, which means chickadees are often found in mixed flocks. Chickadees will also cache food for later use. Their most recognizable call is the "chicka-dee-dee-dee-dee" song, often heard before the bird is seen; the next most common is the "fee-bee, fee-bee" call. Chickadees sometimes gravitate to birch, alder, and willow trees. Perhaps most interesting of all, the chickadee's brain allows neurons and the associated old information to die each fall, in order to free up space to absorb new information and adapt anew to its environment.

Myths, folklore, and cultural associations: Serving as a town crier of sorts in the wild, the chickadee is often seen as bringing news. It is said that if a chickadee perches near your home you will soon hear from a long-lost friend, or that there is a plot afoot against you. Either way, it is a sign to watch for a change of some kind. If you spot a chickadee hanging upside down on a branch, it means that good news is making its way to you. If you hear a chickadee chirping cheerily, good weather is on the horizon.

The chickadee is considered a bold bird, approaching humans and other animals with apparent fearlessness. Some interpret this as a reflection of the chickadee's fabled ability to know the truth about a situation and judge if there is danger inherent in it or not. Because of the chickadee's cheerful song and bouncy flight and general motion, it is often associated with optimism and cheer. As it is one of the first birds to approach a new bird feeder, it is also seen as a trailblazer.

The Mi'kmaq tribe of northeastern North America has a myth involving the chickadee and the constellation Ursa Major, otherwise known as the Big Bear or the Big Dipper. The four stars of the dipper itself represent the bear, and the three stars that make up the handle are the three hunter birds: the first the robin, who functions as the marksman; the second the chickadee, who serves as the cook once the bear is caught; and the last the blue jay, who lags behind gathering firewood. According to the myth the three birds were chasing the bear in the autumn, and the robin shot it with an arrow. The blood splashed and marked the robin's chest with red, as well as splashing some of the leaves of the trees below, which is why some leaves turn red in the fall. As the chickadee cooked the bear, some of the liquefied fat splashed over the edge of the cooking pot, marking some of the leaves with yellow. The blue jay came for the bits left over, as many corvids would do.

The chickadee is the state bird of both Maine and Massachusetts and is the provincial bird of New Brunswick.

Omens and divinatory meaning: The chickadee is a kind of leader within its mixed flock. Ask yourself if your words and actions are impacting a larger group or community than you think. People may be looking to you and your actions for guidance or wisdom. Like the chickadee, you may be a link that draws many different people or social groups together.

The chickadee's willing and natural release of old information every autumn is a valuable lesson. Are you holding on to old patterns, habits, opinions, and beliefs? Is it time to shed them so that you can reexamine current information and situations, and form new opinions and plans? Make it a habit to review your life and views regularly. Remember, shedding outdated information and patterns is healthy and beneficial. You are not the same person you were at this time last year or even this time half a year ago. The world around you changes at a sometimes alarming rate as well. Free yourself up to adapt to it, and you will discover that you can function more efficiently and effectively.

Associated energies: Industry, activity, communication, leadership, unity, playfulness, cheer, adaptability, optimism

Associated seasons: Spring, autumn

Element associations: Air, earth

Color associations: Black, white, gray, brown

Cormorant

Genus: *Phalacrocorax*

Popular and common variants/subspecies/other names: Double-crested cormorant (*Phalacrocorax auritus*), great cormorant (*Phalacrocorax carbo*), shags

Geographic distribution: Cormorant varieties are found in the Pacific, the Atlantic, and the Indian Oceans; in Africa, New Zealand, Australia, and South America; and in subantarctic waters.

Environment: Cormorants are coastal birds, generally considered seawater based, although they are also found inland by freshwater sources.

Physical description: The cormorant is a medium-to-large seabird weighing between 3 and 5 pounds and measuring approximately 30 inches long with a wingspan of approximately 47 inches. The cormorant has mainly dark plumage, although additional coloring is species dependent; most have some sort of white or colored patches on either side of the head. Their feet are webbed; bills are blunt and hooked. The cormorant builds a bulky nest of discarded plant material and human junk. If the bird breeds in a colony, the cormorant chicks will congregate in a social group when they are first able to leave the nest, returning home for meals.

Interesting facts: Cormorants often stand in a pose with their wings partly outstretched, a stance that helps them dry their feathers.

Myths, folklore, and cultural associations: The name *cormorant* comes from the Latin for "raven of the sea," a reference to the inky color of its feathers.

In China and Japan, cormorants were sometimes used as fishing companions. A collar of sorts was tied around the bird's throat, which allowed the bird to swallow only fish smaller than a certain size. If the bird caught a larger fish, it would have to be removed by the fisherman. A cormorant image or talisman is said to bring luck to a fisherman or his vessel. In this respect, a cormorant represents abundance and a successful catch.

The cormorant was often shown in iconography and heraldry in its wings-outstretched pose, reminiscent of Christ on the cross. These birds are therefore associated with nobility and sacrifice. In mockery of this, Milton used the cormorant as one of Satan's disguises in *Paradise Lost*; the cormorant symbolized greed and excess.

In some Scandinavian areas cormorants are considered a good omen; in Norway, the spirits of the deceased lost at sea are thought to come visit their loved ones in the guise of a cormorant. Seeing three cormorants flying together is a message from a dead loved one. If a cormorant alights upon a church steeple in Ireland, it is seen as a bad omen.

Folklore has the cormorant swallowing stones in order to dive deeply enough below the water's surface to catch its meals.

Omens and divinatory meaning: Cormorants lack oil to waterproof their feathers and soak their feathers in order to reduce buoyancy before they dive. This suggests planning ahead and a conscious transition between air and water. The cormorant shows that transitioning back and forth between two states or situations is possible, as long as you prepare correctly and commit yourself fully to one or the other state at any given time.

Cormorants dive to find their food, and their diving action tells us to jump right in, to submerge ourselves fully in whatever we're about to do.

Associated energies: Abundance, commitment

Associated seasons: Spring, summer, fall

Element associations: Air, water

Color association: Black

Crane

Name: Sandhill crane

Species: *Antigone canadensis* (formerly *Grus canadensis*)

Popular and common variants/subspecies/other names: Whooping crane, red-crowned crane, black-crowned crane, blue crane

Geographic distribution: Sandhill cranes are found all over North America, except the northeastern part of Canada and the United States. Crane varieties are found worldwide except in South America and Antarctica.

Environment: Cranes live in wetland areas, such as marshes and bogs, as well as damp grasslands.

Physical description: The crane is a tall bird with a long neck and legs and grayish or white plumage. It measures between 50 and 60 inches long, with a wingspan of between 70 and 80 inches and a weight of approximately 10 to 15 pounds.

Interesting facts: The whooping crane is an endangered species, numbering fewer than 500 in the wild. The more populous sandhill crane is the tallest North American bird. Cranes have highly complicated mating dances, are monogamous, mate for life, and remain in social pairs even outside of breeding season. The crane's typical posture and behavior depict it bending over as it wades to probe into water and mud for food. Cranes will mass to migrate in enormous flocks.

Myths, folklore, and cultural associations: The crane's fidelity and mating rituals make it a common symbol for loyalty and successful marriage. Its fabled long life span also makes it a symbol of longevity.

The crane is a popular symbol in Asian culture, and the practice of folding paper cranes for good fortune, healing, happiness, and success was popularized by Sadako Sasaki, a young victim of the radiation from the Hiroshima disaster. Chains of paper cranes, often numbering a thousand in total, are given as offerings at temples and shrines. The crane is also perceived as a bird capable of flying to the very heavens and is said to have borne spirits of the deceased there upon its back. In ancient China, the crane was used as the symbol of highest-ranking officials.

The longevity of the crane may also have caused it to be associated with a family tree or lineage. The English word *pedigree* may come from the French phrase meaning "foot of the crane": *pied de grue*. Legend has it that the crane's legs grow before its wings do, suggesting that the bird has a strong tie to the ground. The crane is also associated with vigilance; it was said to keep watch on one leg while holding a stone in the other foot. The stone would drop if the crane dozed off, waking it and its companions. Heraldry (the art of designing and displaying coats of arms and other devices that identify a family or group) often shows the crane holding a stone in this way, symbolizing alertness.

In one of Aesop's fables, a peacock laughs at the duller crane. The crane admits that it may not be as visually stunning as the peacock, but it has the capability to soar to the very heavens, whereas the peacock is stuck on the ground. The moral of the story is the commonly repeated adage "Fine feathers do not make fine birds."

In Celtic myth, the crane bag, made from the skin of a crane, held many of the treasures precious to the Irish god Manannan. One of these treasures may have been the staves of ogham, a rune-like system of writing or divination whose shapes are sometimes compared to the thin lines of a crane's legs.

The black-crowned crane is the national bird of Nigeria, and the blue crane is the national bird of South Africa. The red-crowned crane has been nominated as the national bird of China.

Omens and divinatory meaning: If you see a crane flying, it may be drawing your eyes to the heavens, lifting your spirits, and inspiring you to trust in the universe. If you see it standing, it may be advising vigilance and alertness.

Associated energies: Alertness, longevity, success, watchfulness, justice, fidelity

Associated season: Summer

Element associations: Air, water, earth

Color associations: Gray, white

Crow

Name: American crow

Species: *Corvus brachyrhynchos*

Popular and common variants/subspecies/other names:
Common crow, hooded crow (*Corvus cornix*), rook, jackdaw, carrion crow

Geographic distribution: Crows in various forms are found almost worldwide.

Environment: Crows can be found almost anywhere, including in woodland, cities and urban areas, rural areas, and farmland.

Physical description: There are about forty different members of this genus. Crows are generally recognized by their glossy black plumage, black beaks, and black legs. The American crow measures approximately 17 inches long, with a wingspan of about 35 inches and a weight averaging 16 ounces.

Interesting facts: Crows are classified among the world's most intelligent creatures, being capable of not only tool use but of tool improvisation or construction. They also engage in play, both with one another and with other bird species.

Myths, folklore, and cultural associations: The word *cunning* could have been created for the Corvidae family. Crows are adaptive, intelligent, and abundant; they are found pretty much everywhere in all kinds of habitats. They are also very social creatures. We use the phrase "as the crow flies" to describe a direct path, a reference to the crow's ability to go anywhere and do anything.

Most crows eat carrion; they do not kill. Rather, they dine on the remains of animals, or the leftovers of other predators. Crows waste nothing. They serve an important function in the cycle of life, cleaning up and contributing to the easier decomposition of a corpse. This behavior associates them with death in general, as a prophesier of doom and war. In fact, the collective noun for a group of crows is a *murder* of crows.

Crows are often associated with gods and goddesses of war. This is, no doubt, a direct link to the presence of crows at battlefields, ready to dine upon the dead. A classic example of this is the Irish battle goddess the Morrigan, a triple-aspected deity composed of three separate goddesses: Nemain, Badb, and Macha. Badb, in particular, was associated with crows and was said to be able to take the form of a crow to fly over a battlefield.

The relationship with war and death also underlies the crow's connection to the Otherworld. The crow is sometimes perceived as a harbinger of death as well. The Scots have an expression for death: "going away up the Crow Road." This may be a reference to the folk belief that crows serve as psychopomps, or guides between the world of the living and the afterlife. In Hindu belief, crows serve as intermediaries who bring offerings of food and water to deceased ancestors on the anniversary of the relative's death, a practice of expressing gratitude known as sraddha. In ancient Egypt, however, the crow was a symbol of faithful love because of the bird's monogamous nature. In Chinese and Japanese mythology, crows are sometimes used as symbols for filial duty.

One of the most famous tales from *Aesop's Fables* is that of "The Crow and the Pitcher." A crow, half dead with thirst, discovers a jug that has only a little bit of water left in it. Unable to reach the water by sticking his head inside, the crow thinks for a moment, then picks up a pebble and drops it into the jug. He repeats this action over and over until the level of the water has risen to the brim of the jug, allowing him to dip his beak in and drink. The moral encoded in the fable teaches that one can accomplish a seemingly impossible task with a series of small actions. However, the story also illustrates the crow's ability to problem solve and use what tools are at hand to achieve a specific purpose.

Omens and divinatory meaning: How canny are you? How inventive can you be when faced with a seemingly insurmountable challenge? The crow urges you to think outside the box, to examine what tools and skills you have at your disposal, and to apply them in perhaps unconventional ways to achieve your goals.

The crow teaches you about change. Change is not to be feared; it is part of the natural course of things. The death or end of one thing signifies the birth or beginning of another. Crows teach you about cycles too. They are carrion birds, and they help you to remember that even in death there is something that feeds life. Death is not loss; it is transformation. The crow is also a psychopomp, thus prompting you to think about your connections to the Otherworld. Is your perception of death healthy, or is it problematic? As a psychopomp, the crow accompanies spirits through what many of us see as a difficult journey or change. If you are having trouble handling some sort of change in your life, call on the crow to be your companion through it.

The crow, like the raven, is often portrayed as a trickster figure in Native American mythology. The crow reminds you to have fun while you're working to understand life and how you fit into the cosmos, which can too often be an overly serious enterprise. Are you denying yourself the opportunity to play?

Associated energies: Death, prophecy, change, play, innovation

Associated seasons: All seasons

Element associations: Earth, air

Color associations: Black, purple

Cuckoo

Name: Yellow-billed cuckoo

Species: *Coccyzus americanus*

Popular and common variants/subspecies/other names: Black-billed cuckoo, common or European cuckoo (*Cuculus canorus*)

Geographic distribution: The yellow-billed cuckoo lives and migrates from the southern United States down through Mexico and Central America to winter in the upper two-thirds of South America. Cuckoos can be found in all continents except Antarctica.

Environment: Cuckoos prefer open woodland with a thick layer of underbrush or scrub, often with a source of water nearby.

Physical description: A slender, medium-sized songbird, the yellow-billed cuckoo has a dark brownish/black/gray back and wings, and a cream or white front. The upper part of the bill is black, and the lower part is yellow. The cuckoo measures approximately 11 inches long, with a wingspan of 16 inches and a weight of approximately 2 ounces.

Interesting facts: The cuckoo is a shy bird whose call is more often noticed than the bird itself. Cuckoo hatchlings develop incredibly quickly; only about seventeen days elapse between the time the egg is laid and the fledgling leaves the nest. The hatchlings become feathered within two hours of hatching.

The cuckoo is a brood parasite, meaning that it lays its eggs in the nests of other birds, often pushing out one of the resident eggs in order to replace it. If the cuckoo chick hatches before the resident chicks it will often push them out of the nest. The cuckoo can mimic the calls of the resident hatchlings.

Myths, folklore, and cultural associations: The cuckoo is the stereotypical bird that leaps to mind when we think of parasitic activity. The term "cuckoo's child" is a phrase we use for a changeling of some kind. We also say that someone is "cuckoo" for something if she is obsessed with it, or if she is a fool. If someone has been deceived in the marital bed, we say he has been "cuckolded" ("old cuckoo"); in other words, someone else has been figuratively laying eggs in his nest.

The cuckoo is one of the birds associated with Hera, the Greek goddess of marriage and women. Zeus turned himself into a cuckoo to woo her.

Celtic mythology tells us that the cuckoo's call can summon the souls of the dead and that the bird itself could travel between the worlds. Cuckoos were also said to have the power of prophecy, specifically regarding the length of one's life. The cuckoo's call was one of the harbingers of spring in Europe, immortalized in a Middle English song that is one of the earliest examples of counterpoint, "Sumer is icumen in, Lhude sing cuccu!" ("Summer has come in, Loudly sing, cuckoo!").

In American folklore, for some people hearing a cuckoo's call means that a storm is on the way. For others, the direction from which they hear the call provides meaning: from the north, sorrow is coming; from the south, a death is foretold; from the east, comfort is on the way; and from the west, good luck will come.

Omens and divinatory meaning: The cuckoo can be a sign that you need to pay more attention to your relationship with the dead. What can your ancestors or recently lost loved ones teach you?

The cuckoo may also carry a message to be aware of deceit. Is someone not being entirely truthful with you? Is someone perhaps taking credit for something that you have done or using your work without permission or attribution?

Finally, the cuckoo may advise you to be heard rather than seen.

Associated energies: Prophecy, the Otherworld, change, transformation, fertility, long life

Associated seasons: Spring, summer

Element association: Air

Color associations: Gray, black, brown, cream, white

Dove

Family: Columbidae

Popular and common variants/subspecies/other names:
Mourning dove (*Zenaida macroura*), ring-necked dove (*Streptopelia capicola*), ground dove (*Columbina passerina*)

Geographic distribution: Doves are found worldwide except in the high Arctic, Antarctica, the Sahara Desert, and other harsh places. Most live in tropical or subtropical climates.

Environment: Doves prefer woodland, forested areas, and fields.

Physical description: Doves are medium-sized birds with short, stout bodies, short necks, and short beaks. Size varies according to the species, as does coloring. The mourning dove, the most common species in North America, measures about 11 inches long, with a wingspan of 18 inches and a weight of approximately 5 ounces.

Interesting facts: Doves produce a milky substance in their gullets with which to feed their young; to eat it, the chick puts its head inside the adult's mouth. The typical call of the dove is a low coo, sometimes characterized as a mournful cry.

Myths, folklore, and cultural associations: Stereotypically, the dove is portrayed as white and gentle, sweet and loving. The dove is a symbol of the Holy Spirit in Christian iconography. Some iconographers show Mary being blessed by a dove at the moment of Annunciation, and Jesus was blessed by the Holy Spirit in the form of a dove at his baptism. The dove is said to be so pure that it is the one form into which Satan cannot transform himself. Doves and pigeons were the only birds suitable for sacrifice by the Hebrews, according to Leviticus 1:14. The dove appears as a symbol of purity on the Holy Grail in Thomas Malory's *Morte d'Arthur*. In Muslim lore, a dove murmured the words of God into the ear of Muhammad.

Today the dove is a symbol of peace, often portrayed with an olive branch in its mouth. This iconography is taken from the story of Noah releasing the bird to bring back proof that there was land again somewhere and that the floodwaters were receding. The dove is also seen as representing love; it was a symbol of Aphrodite, the Greek goddess of love, and of Venus, her Roman counterpart. Lovers are said to "bill and coo" like doves. The dove is a monogamous bird, which may be the source of its connection with romantic and eternal love.

In Slavic folklore, doves were believed to conduct the souls of the dead to heaven. For the Celts, the mournful call of a dove meant the peaceful passing of someone.

Omens and divinatory meaning: Doves call you to regain your serenity. Do you feel off balance or out of step with the world? Are you harried or frazzled? The dove reminds you to take a deep breath and release all your tension and stress.

The dove also urges you to look at your relationships with your partner(s)—romantic, work related, or otherwise. Are you in harmony with them? Is there friction? Reach out and smooth over any rough spots. Seeing a dove may be an omen of a new relationship or a shift in an existing one.

Doves are also associated with purity and innocence. Do you feel as if life has jaded you? Try to recapture a sense of innocence, of wonder and love for the world around you. Operating constantly with a cynical worldview is exhausting. In a situation that is frustrating or upsetting to you, a dove may be encouraging you to wipe the slate clean and start again.

As a symbol of the Holy Spirit, the dove is associated with the mystical fifth element of spirit. Let your sighting of a dove remind you to reconnect with the spiritual aspect of your life; accept it as a blessing.

Associated energies: Peace, love, serenity, blessing, patience, grace, hope, marital happiness, purity

Associated seasons: All seasons

Element associations: Air, water, earth

Color associations: White, ivory, buff, brown, gray

Duck

Family: Anatidae

Popular and common variants/subspecies/other names: Domesticated duck, mallard, wood duck, Muscovy duck, American wigeon

Geographic distribution: Ducks are found everywhere in the world except Antarctica.

Environment: Ducks prefer a variety of environments depending on the species, but they can generally be found in wooded areas, by waterways, swampland, marshes, parks, and other cultured or landscaped areas.

Physical description: One of the duck's identifying features is its webbed feet. Its legs are set far back on its body, making it slightly awkward on land (and creating that characteristic waddle many people find amusing), but ducks are very smooth and powerful in the water. Size ranges according to species, but as an example, mallards measure approximately 23 inches long with an average weight of 2.5 pounds; wood ducks measure approximately 20 inches long and weigh just over a pound. Many species have round heads, rounded but flattish bills, and short tails. Plumage varies between dappled brown to patches of strong color on the wings, breast, or head.

Interesting facts: Mostly water-based birds, ducks can be found on both saltwater and freshwater. The word *duck* means to stoop or bend down, descriptive of the behavior ducks display when dabbling, or dipping their heads underwater to feed. Most ducks in northern areas migrate to warmer climates for the winter, but those in comfortable temperate climates remain there all year round. Ducks are considered game birds in many areas. Like chickens, ducks are domesticated for their meat and eggs. Domesticated ducks require access to water in order to survive. When a duck's eggs hatch, the mother leads the ducklings immediately to the nearest body of water. Eider ducks are specifically bred for their plentiful, soft down and lend their name to the *eiderdown*, a word for a feather quilt.

Myths, folklore, and cultural associations: In both China and Japan, a pair of Mandarin ducks symbolizes wedded fidelity and happiness, because Mandarins are among the few species of duck that mate for life. The Mandarin duck can also be used as a symbol with which to work on problematic relationships.

A statue found in northern France depicts the Celtic goddess Sequana standing in a duck-shaped boat, perhaps a nod to the duck's ability to navigate waterways, or perhaps to its association with fertility and feminine virtues. In Egyptian hieroglyphs, the duck symbol represents "son." Additionally, the flying duck hieroglyph literally means "to fly."

To hear a duck quacking is said to be a good omen, particularly in regard to prosperity. To see one fly is also a good omen, for it offers hope and signifies that you will rise out of whatever difficulty you may be experiencing.

Omens and divinatory meaning: Seeing a duck can alert you literally or figuratively to duck, to keep your head down and stay out of the way for a little while. Something may be coming that could ruffle your feathers or disturb your customary smooth sailing. Alternatively, a duck sighting may prompt you to look at your responsibilities: Are you trying to duck out on anything? If you're handling something complicated, are you sure that you have "all your ducks in a row"?

A duck's physical shape and webbed feet help it stay afloat and navigate waters with ease. The energy of the duck may help you keep afloat and enable you to go with the flow. Tap its buoyancy to bob atop rough waters.

Associated energies: Weathering storms and crises, emotional balance, transition, wisdom, sensitivity, simplicity, hearth and home, partnership

Associated season: Fall

Element associations: Water, earth, air

Color associations: White, brown, teal, black, green

Eagle

Order: Falconiformes

Family: Accipitridae

Popular and common variants/subspecies/other names: Bald eagle, golden eagle

Geographic distribution: Eagle species are mainly found in Africa and Eurasia, with a handful found in Australia and North, Central, and South America. The bald eagle can be found across North America, ranging from northern Canada down through the southern United States.

Environment: Eagles are found on cliffs in coastal areas, mountainous regions, and prairies.

Physical description: Eagles are large, heavy birds of prey with strong hooked beaks, muscular legs, and talons. The bald eagle has a brown body with white head and tail, whereas the golden eagle has an all-brown body with a golden iridescence on the head. Eagles measure approximately 32 inches long, with a wingspan of 80 inches and a weight of about 9 to 10 pounds.

Interesting facts: Eagles build nests called eyries high on cliffs. They have excellent eyesight, which enables them to soar high above the ground and still spy prey. Their strong wings allow them to remain aloft for extended periods of time and to change altitude rapidly. After being threatened with extinction, the relocation of breeding pairs of bald eagles from Canada and governmental protections have increased this species' population in the United States.

Myths, folklore, and cultural associations: Of all birds, the eagle has one of the longest life spans at an average of about twenty-five years. This may have been the source of an enduring myth of renewal, which told that aging eagles would fly high into the sky until they reached the sun, where they would fling themselves into the solar flame. They would then plunge down to a body of water and throw themselves in, emerging rejuvenated. The eagle's penchant for flying high in the sky also makes it a solar symbol.

The eagle is frequently used as a symbol of power, especially military power, and the bird is often associated with gods. The eagle appears on the coats of arms of several nations, including Egypt, Austria, Poland, and Armenia. The golden eagle is the national bird of Scotland, Germany, and Mexico. The Great Seal of the United States features a bald eagle.

The eagle is the symbol of Saint John the Evangelist, and church lecterns are sometimes decorated with eagles in his honor. In Christian iconography, the eagle often represents resurrection and renewal.

Omens and divinatory meaning: An eagle can indicate keen sight of some kind. Is there something that you need to "keep an eagle eye out" for? Are you losing sight of the details? Do you need a better overview of things? Are little things escaping your perception?

The eagle may also bring a message that it's time to return to your responsibilities or to reassert your power. Have you become too lax? Are you assigning too many responsibilities to others and weakening your control over things that are ultimately your responsibility? There is a fine balance between micromanaging and effective delegation. The eagle is a symbol of leadership; it may guide you to reestablish your leadership and to remind people that you are in charge. The eagle may also be urging you to reinvent yourself, to experience a renewal or rebirth.

Associated energies: Renewal, perception, power, leadership, longevity

Associated season: Summer

Element associations: Air, fire

Color associations: White, black, yellow, brown

Egret

Name: Great egret

Species: *Ardea alba*

Popular and common variants/subspecies/other names: Snowy egret

Geographic distribution: The great egret is found from southern Canada down through the United States and South America, as well as in Europe, Australia, Africa, and Asia. Partially migratory, northern birds will move southward during the cooler times of year.

Environment: The egret lives in wetlands such as marshes and swamps, in both saltwater and freshwater, and along rivers and ponds. It is comfortable in close contact with human civilization.

Physical description: The great egret is a long-necked and long-legged bird with white plumage. The bill is yellow, and the legs black. It measures 35 to 40 inches long, with a wingspan of about 55 inches and a weight of about 2 pounds.

Interesting facts: A kind of heron, the egret has a slow, measured flight during which it pulls its head back instead of extending it. The egret lives and breeds in colonies. A wading bird, the egret will spear small frogs and fish with its long, thin beak.

Myths, folklore, and cultural associations: Formerly called *aigettes* ("little herons"), these stately birds were once in great demand by the millinery trade for their feathers. As such, the egret is now the symbol of the US's National Audubon Society, whose tenets include protecting birds from being killed to harvest their feathers.

To the Maori, the indigenous people of New Zealand, an egret is a symbol of the ultimate in rarity and beauty. To see one is a great blessing, as egrets are rare in New Zealand.

(See also Heron, Stork.)

Omens and divinatory meaning: An egret conveys a message of serenity and beauty. A noble bird, it reminds us to stand tall and to be self-possessed.

The Maori perception of the egret as a thing of rarity is also to be considered. Every moment of a day is sacred and beautiful in some way. Are you missing that? Are you so buried in work or daily cares that you're forgetting to lift your head and look around you, to soak in the beauty that abides in this stressful, chaotic world?

Associated energies: Stability, beauty

Associated season: Summer

Element associations: Air, water, earth

Color association: White

Falcon

Name: Peregrine falcon

Popular and common variants/subspecies/other names: Peregrine (*Falco peregrinus*), merlin (*Falco columbarius*), gyrfalcon (*Falco rusticolus*)

Geographic distribution: Falcons are found on all continents except Antarctica.

Environment: Falcons are found in mountainous areas and open woodland, though they are at ease in urban areas and often substitute skyscrapers for cliffs.

Physical description: The falcon has a curve at the end of its beak that is sometimes referred to as a hook. Peregrine falcons average

17 inches in length, with a wingspan of about 42 inches and an average weight of about 2.5 pounds.

Interesting facts: Falcon refers to any species within the genus *Falco*. Falcons have a very specific dive called a stoop during which they pause in the air, then arrow downward swiftly to seize their prey. Peregrine falcons have been recorded flying at speeds of approximately 200 mph in these stoops, although regular flying speeds average 30 mph and increase to approximately 65 mph in pursuit of prey. Like eagles, falcons have an incredibly precise sense of sight. Male peregrine falcons are smaller than the females.

Myths, folklore, and cultural associations: One of the older names for falcons was *tiercel*, meaning "third," as it was thought that only one egg in three hatched a male bird (falconers still refer to a male falcon as a tiercel).

The falcon was one of the forms associated with the Egyptian god Horus, the god of war and hunting, and the Eye of Horus talisman (correctly known as the Wedjat), which represents the all-seeing eye of both the bird and the god. The hieroglyph of a falcon refers directly to Horus and means "that which is above." Freya, the Norse goddess of love and sexuality, owned a falcon-feather cloak with which she shapeshifted and flew.

Falconry, the sport of hunting game with trained small birds of prey, was an enormously popular social sport in medieval Europe. The falcon is sometimes used as a symbol of freedom from bondage or slavery, referring to a falcon that escapes the keeper's hand and flies free, never to return. Likewise, the falcon can symbolize unfettered or passionate love, building on the image of a tamed falcon, once unhooded and untied, bursting forth in pursuit of its goal.

(See also Hawk, Kestrel.)

Omens and divinatory meaning: The falcon is power in a small package. These birds move efficiently in more than one sense of the word, wasting no energy or motion. How is your efficiency these days? You may need to work on your split-second decision-making.

Peregrine means wanderer. If you see a peregrine falcon, it may be reminding you that movement is important. This doesn't necessarily mean that you're about to pull up stakes and move to another place (although it might), but it may suggest that clinging to the familiar can be limiting. Being too comfortable and not seeking to expand your horizons can have a negative impact on your potential. Try pushing yourself outside your comfort zone in order to expose yourself to new ideas and concepts.

The falcon can be seen as a diurnal symbol, as it is generally associated with the sun. Remember, though, that the Egyptian god Horus had two eyes: one was the sun, but the other was the moon. Thus, the falcon can be a symbol of balance and completion too.

Associated energies: Perception, efficiency, power, balance

Associated seasons: Summer, fall

Element associations: Air, fire

Color associations: Brown, buff, cream, rust

Finch

Name: House finch

Species: *Carpodacus mexicanus*

Popular and common variants/subspecies/other names: Chaffinch, bullfinch, grosbeak

Geographic distribution: Finches are found in every continent except Australia, the Arctic, and Antarctica. Most finch species are located in the Southern Hemisphere. The house finch is found in the eastern and western United States and south through Mexico.

Environment: Depending on the species, finches can be found in woodland, mountains, or even deserts.

Physical description: Finches are generally small birds with strong, stubby beaks. The house finch measures approximately 5 inches long, with a wingspan of about 8 inches and a weight of 0.75 ounce. The bird's plumage is mostly brown and it has a rosy chest and head.

Interesting facts: Finches have a bouncy flight consisting of alternating sequences of wing flaps and gliding. They are gregarious, and they build hanging, basket-like nests.

Myths, folklore, and cultural associations: Finches are often kept as pets for their pretty plumage and chirpy calls, and therefore they can symbolize domesticity, beauty, and mastery over nature. Finches, like other small birds such as sparrows, often represented souls or spirits in Christian iconography.

Colorado's state bird is sometimes called the prairie lark finch, which is actually the lark bunting, a member of the sparrow family.

(See also Goldfinch, Lark.)

Omens and divinatory meaning: If you see a finch, examine your level of activity. Have you been trying to juggle so much that you're wearing yourself out, leaving you frazzled and harried? Perhaps you're mismanaging your energy, putting too much into areas of your life that aren't nourishing you in return. Remember to balance activity with rest, and that includes mental rest as well. Just because you don't physically run around to get stuff done doesn't mean you're not wearing yourself out by running overtime in a mental exercise wheel.

Associated energies: Activity, vitality

Associated season: Summer

Element association: Air

Color associations: Brown, red

Flamingo

Species: *Phoenicopterus ruber* (American flamingo)

Popular and common variants/subspecies/other names: Caribbean flamingo, American/West Indian flamingo, greater flamingo, lesser flamingo

Geographic distribution: You'll find flamingos in Africa, southern Europe and Asia, and South America; the American flamingo can specifically be found in Florida.

Environment: Flamingos prefer shallow inland lakes and rivers, and mudflats.

Physical description: A tall, thin, graceful wading bird, the flamingo can reach heights of more than 5 feet and weighs about 7 pounds. The long, slim neck and legs make up much of this bird's height. Juvenile flamingos are gray; their plumage turns pink or reddish as a result of ingesting certain bacteria and carotenes along with their food. Captive flamingos may need vitamin supplements in order to maintain their characteristic color.

Interesting facts: The flamingo often stands on one leg with the other tucked up under its body, which may allow it to conserve body heat more efficiently. Flamingos are very social birds, living in flocks and colonies of hundreds.

Both parents build the foot-high nest and nurse chicks from milk produced in their crops—expanded, muscular pouches found near the throat—and regurgitated into the chick's mouth. The flamingo feeds by turning its head upside down in water and rotating it back and forth in semicircles to sieve through the water for tiny creatures.

Myths, folklore, and cultural associations: It's said that the English name for the flamingo is possibly derived from the Latin *flamma*, or "flame." It has also been suggested that the flamingo, with its bright plumage, was one of the possible birds proposed as the mythical phoenix or firebird, a bird that lives between 500 and 1,000 years before bursting into flame and burning itself to ashes, from which is born a new phoenix hatchling or a phoenix egg.

In ancient Egypt, flamingos were believed to be living representations of the gods, and they were worshipped in Peru.

The unfortunate flamingos of Wonderland were used as croquet mallets in Lewis Carroll's *Alice's Adventures in Wonderland*.

Omens and divinatory meaning: What was the flamingo doing when you saw it? If it was wading with its head in the water, sieving for food, that motion suggests that you should carefully sift through any current situation to find the truth of the matter. If the flamingo you saw was standing in its characteristic one-legged stance, it may be indicating that you should rest and conserve energy.

The one-legged stance also advises you to address the concept of balance in your life. Are you devoting too much energy or attention to one area of your life at the expense of others?

Is your health at risk because you're focusing too strongly on your career? Moderation in all things is a good rule of thumb.

As the flamingo breeding pair works together to build the nest and care for the hatchlings, perhaps you should also examine your current division of labor and responsibilities with your partner or colleagues. Is everyone carrying his or her share of the load?

Associated energies: Grace, thoroughness, cooperation, balance

Associated season: Summer

Element associations: Water, air

Color associations: Pink, orange, red, coral, scarlet, white, gray

Goldfinch

Name: American goldfinch

Species: *Spinus tristis*

Popular and common variants/subspecies/other names: European goldfinch, lesser goldfinch, Lawrence's goldfinch

Geographic distribution: The American goldfinch is found across southern Canada in the summer, in the northern United States year round, and in the southern United States and eastern Mexico in the winter. The European goldfinch (*Carduelis carduelis*) is native to Europe, North Africa, and western and central Asia.

Environment: The goldfinch's preferred environments include meadows, fields, open woodland, and floodplains. This bird is very comfortable in cultivated and urban residential areas.

Physical description: The goldfinch is a small, stubby bird measuring about 4.5 inches long, with a wingspan of approximately 8 inches and a weight of roughly half an ounce. The bird's plumage is mostly bright yellow, and it has a black blaze above the beak, black wing edges touched with white, and a white rump. The female is a duller color in the summer, but in the winter the male dulls whereas the female brightens slightly.

Interesting facts: The goldfinch molts twice a year, in spring and fall. They breed later than other finches, nesting in June or July. Unlike many other small birds, the goldfinch is almost exclusively vegetarian; insects do not form an intentional part of its diet.

Myths, folklore, and cultural associations: The word *carduelis* in the European goldfinch's name (*Carduelis carduelis*) means "thistle-eating," and goldfinches love weeds such as thistles, particularly milkweed and other plants that produce flossy or fluffy seed heads. The goldfinch eats the seeds of these plants and uses the silky fluff of the plant to line and weave into its nest. The European goldfinch was sometimes called a thistle finch, and this bird is the *distelfink* seen in the folk art and lore of the Pennsylvania Dutch in the United States. The distelfink represents happiness and good fortune to this community.

The gold color of this bird connects it with wealth. If the first bird a girl saw on Valentine's Day was a goldfinch, she would marry a wealthy man. The goldfinch was also believed to be a symbol of protection against the plague in medieval times.

The American goldfinch, or eastern goldfinch, is the official bird of the US states Iowa, New Jersey, and Washington. Goldfinches are sometimes casually referred to as wild canaries.

The collective noun for a group of goldfinches is a *charm*, which is a lovely word suggesting the bird's association with luck, health, joy, and wealth.

Omens and divinatory meaning: Yellow is a color of joy, cheer, and health. Seeing a goldfinch can be a boost to your general well-being. It may also be a sign to consciously introduce more joy into your life by engaging in what you love to do more than you currently are doing.

The male goldfinch's bright colors fade after the summer and become a more subdued olive brown, whereas the female's plumage brightens in the fall. This can be a reminder that you can choose your season to shine. Not everyone can be in the spotlight all the time; it can be draining and unhealthy. But by choosing your time carefully, you can make a significant impact. Just remember that in order to balance that season of shining, you need to retreat again and allow others their time in the light as well.

Associated energies: Joy, happiness, health, abundance, prosperity

Associated season: Summer

Element association: Air

Color associations: Yellow, black, brown

Goose

Order: Anseriformes

Family: Anatidae

Popular and common variants/subspecies/other names: Snow goose, gray goose, Canada goose, domestic goose (*Anser anser domesticus* or *Anser cygnoides*)

Geographic distribution: Domestic and wild geese are found worldwide.

Environment: Geese live in marshes, swamps, riversides, parks, and barnyards.

Physical description: Geese are large waterfowl with long necks, large bodies, short tails, and webbed feet. Domestic geese are white or gray. They tend to have heavier rear ends than wild geese, which somewhat limits their flight capability.

Interesting facts: We tend to laugh at geese, thinking them silly creatures, but there's more than meets the eye to this bird. Geese tend to serve as unofficial defense in a barnyard, as they are aggressive birds, and it's not at all funny to be chased by one. Geese are technically waterfowl but spend lots of time on land, wading and walking in their search for food. Wild geese fly more than domestic geese do. In fact, one of the signs of spring or fall is hearing or seeing skeins of geese flying past on their migratory journey.

Myths, folklore, and cultural associations: Like chickens and ducks, geese are among the world's most commonly domesticated birds, kept for their eggs, meat, and feathers. A domesticated goose can lay up to fifty eggs a year, and therefore the goose is often associated with fertility and fecundity. In a fairy tale about a goose who laid golden eggs, its greedy owner grew impatient with the daily gold and killed the goose to access what he expected to be a treasure trove. Instead, all he got was a dead goose. The story's moral is that patience is its own reward.

The Norse goddess Freya was said to be goose-footed, and sacred geese guarded the temple of Juno in ancient Rome. The white goose is also associated with Aphrodite, the Greek goddess of love.

The tales of Mother Goose, the mythical creator of a collection of nursery rhymes, are actually a translation of the stories by the fictional storyteller from Charles Perrault's seventeenth-century work *Contes de ma mère l'Oye* (*Tales of My Mother the Goose*). The name Mother Goose may have been inspired by the French queen Bertha, called "Goose-foot," mother of Charlemagne and a patron of children. The goose was also a sacred bird of Holda, a Germanic goddess.

Omens and divinatory meaning: If you see a goose, you should examine several areas in your life. Abundance of some kind may be coming your way (and remember, abundance doesn't always mean wealth). You might become more watchful for an attack of some kind, small or significant, and think about what is precious to you in order to protect it. Finally, take a look at your current passions, obsessions, or hobbies. Are you on a wild goose chase about something? Have you thought out your path and plan of attack carefully? What's your focus? Have you collected as much information and data as possible to make a balanced and informed decision? Do you have a clearly defined goal?

Canada geese share leadership roles in their migratory flights, trading off the point position. Take a moment to look at how you work within a team. Can you step up and assume a leadership position when necessary, and then step back again when someone else's strengths would better serve the group's needs? The migratory aspect of geese could indicate upcoming travel.

Associated energies: Fecundity, protection, domesticity, teamwork, travel

Associated seasons: Spring, fall

Element associations: Air, water, earth

Color associations: White, brown, gray

Grackle

Name: Common grackle

Species: *Quiscalis quiscula*

Popular and common variants/subspecies/other names: Great-tailed grackle, boat-tailed grackle

Geographic distribution: In North America, the grackle is found in eastern and central Canada and in the United States as far south as Florida. Species of grackle are found through Mexico and Central and South America.

Environment: Grackles are found in agricultural areas, cultivated residential areas, forest edges, meadows, and marshes.

Physical description: The common grackle is a blackbird that measures about 12 inches long, weighs about 4 ounces, and has a wingspan of approximately 16 inches. The plumage is an iridescent black, shining with green, purple, bronze, and/or blue highlights.

Interesting facts: The grackle often nests in colonies and flocks with other blackbirds. The grackle forages in open ground, walking through grass in populated areas, searching or waiting for food, or sometimes aggressively taking it from other birds. For this reason grackles are often unwelcome at backyard bird feeders. They are considered destructive in large groups, damaging crops and spreading garbage. They are also noted for the amount of noise they make when in a group, and for their guttural, rusty, croaking call.

Myths, folklore, and cultural associations: The English name for this bird comes from *gracula*, Latin for "small jackdaw." Grackles are sometimes casually referred to as purple jackdaws, because of the purple sheen to their iridescent feathers. A casual collective name for a group of these birds is a *plague* of grackles, which suggests their unwelcome presence.

Folklore has it that there will be one more snowfall after the grackles return to a region in spring.

(See also Blackbird, Crow, Raven.)

Omens and divinatory meaning: If you see a grackle, examine how you've been behaving toward other people. Have you been taking advantage of them? Have you been riding roughshod over them, unaware of the destruction you're leaving behind?

Think, too, about how noisy you've been. Have you been talking a lot and not saying much of substance? Have you been chattering with a group of people, either online or in real life, and not really putting your money where your mouth is?

Sometimes, though, we need to be loud and aggressive in order to survive, to get what we need in order to accomplish what must be done. In this case, the grackle can symbolize gritty determination and dedication.

The grackle's iridescent plumage can also be associated with illusion and the capability of dazzling or redirecting people. You have to concentrate to see past the shiny reflection into the grackle's darkness. In this, the grackle can also represent focus and dedication and spiritual self-examination.

Associated energies: Determination, aggression, illusion

Associated season: Spring

Element associations: Air, earth

Color associations: Black, with bronze, purple, blue, and green highlights

Grouse

Order: Galliformes

Family: Phasianidae

Popular and common variants/subspecies/other names: Ruffed grouse, red grouse, rock ptarmigan, willow ptarmigan, prairie chicken

Geographic distribution: Most grouse are located in temperate and subarctic zones of the Northern Hemisphere.

Environment: The grouse prefers wooded areas with available undergrowth.

Physical description: Heavier and thicker than a chicken, grouse have elaborate plumage, including feathered legs and feet, and a crest on the head. Their coloring tends toward gray and brown, designed to blend into the forest floor. Some species have red cheeks (wattles, similar to turkeys). The ruffed grouse measures about 17 inches long, has a wingspan of about 22 inches, and weighs roughly 1.5 pounds.

Interesting facts: The grouse lays eggs until its clutch is large enough to incubate. Then the eggs all hatch together at once.

Myths, folklore, and cultural associations: The grouse's status as a game bird and as common prey in the natural food chain make it a staple in the diets of many predators such as owls, falcons, foxes, and coyotes. Although the bird is plentiful, its excellent camouflage makes it a challenge to hunt.

The grouse is known for its courtship dance, during which it often spirals or circles, while impressively displaying crest, ruff, and tail feathers. The grouse's dance calls to mind the sacred dances of shamans and Native American culture.

Folklore says that a pregnant woman should not eat grouse meat, or she may have a stillborn child. The feathers of the ptarmigan are said to ward off lightning. If the feathered toe fringes on a grouse are thicker than usual, it is said to foretell a heavy winter.

The black grouse's feathers are a traditional element of hats belonging to traditional outfits of some European cultural groups, such as Scotland and Alpine cultures. The ruffed grouse is also the official game bird of the US state of Pennsylvania.

Omens and divinatory meaning: The grouse is quiet and invisible until provoked. At that time, it bursts forth from its quiet camouflage, startling an unaware passerby. How did you spy the grouse? Was it quiet and invisible, meaning you spied it through its camouflage, or did you see it only after it burst forth in a flurry of feathers? If the former, then your perception is keen, and you will have good fortune seeing details that may pass others by in important situations. If the latter, the grouse may be telling you that you're not paying close enough attention to what is right before your eyes. Someone may be trying to slip under your radar, hoping to not be noticed.

Associated energies: Movement, stillness, life cycle

Associated season: Autumn

Element associations: Air, earth

Color associations: Brown, black, white

Gull

Name: American herring gull

Species: *Larus smithsonianus*

Popular and common variants/subspecies/other names: Swallow-tailed gull, laughing gull, Franklin's gull, ring-billed gull, California gull, tern, European herring gull (*Larus argentatus*)

Geographic distribution: Species of gull are found on all continents, including the high Arctic and parts of Antarctica.

Environment: Although our first instinct is to look for gulls along coasts of rivers and lakes, these birds are also frequently found inland around food sources such as garbage dumps.

Physical description: The American herring gull is a medium-sized bird with gray-and-white plumage, a yellow bill, and webbed feet. The common gull measures approximately 24 inches long, with a wingspan of approximately 55 inches and an average weight of 36 ounces.

Interesting facts: Seagulls are omnivores. They'll scavenge for food but are also bold enough to snatch it from other animals and even humans. They flock in large groups and nest in colonies. Their slightly melancholy cry is easily recognizable; gulls were called mews in the Middle Ages because of their cry. Some calls sound more like a mocking laugh.

Myths, folklore, and cultural associations: The gull is colloquially known as the seagull, but gulls are found inland as well as in coastal regions, near freshwater as well as saltwater. They are very adaptable birds.

"Gull" is the root of the word *gullible*. If you believe something untrue or incredible you are a gull, possibly because you'll figuratively swallow just about anything, as the bird literally will.

Fishermen used to watch for flocks of gulls to indicate the presence of shoals of fish. In general, we tend to associate gulls with the idea of freedom. Their cries usually figure in relaxing memories of beach visits or seaside holidays. Watching gulls wheel and soar in the air high above us can be an inspiring sight, evoking peace or longing.

One of the more famous seagulls in literature is the titular character of *Jonathan Livingston Seagull* by Richard Bach, a spiritual fable about a seagull who wishes to rise above the petty daily life of a gull and to become an accomplished flyer, symbolically rising above the lowest common denominator. This story has also helped firmly fix the association between gulls and freedom in the mind of the modern birder.

Omens and divinatory meaning: The gull is an adaptable scavenger. Are you using your resources to their utmost potential? Should you be thinking outside the box and developing a use or application for an item or piece of information that didn't seem to fit?

Think about the juxtaposition between the seagull's association with freedom with the reaction we often have of disgust and our perception of the bird as a nuisance when encountered in daily life. Does the seagull make you uncomfortable? Meditate upon the apparent contradiction and the discomfort. If you see the seagull as a pest, try to see beyond that to the freedom it represents. If you see it as a noble symbol of liberty, remember that it has baser associations too. Consider whether you interpret the gull's call as being reminiscent of laughter or something sad. The gull reminds us that everything has a flip side.

The gull may also have appeared to caution you against becoming someone's gull. Are you easily fooled, or gullible? Take everything with a grain of salt and think carefully about what you accept as truth.

Associated energies: Balance, adaptability, freedom

Associated season: Summer

Element associations: Air, water

Color associations: White, gray, yellow

Hawk

Order: Accipitriformes

Family: Accipitridae

Popular and common variants/subspecies/other names: Northern harrier, red-tailed hawk, northern goshawk, red-shouldered hawk, sparrowhawk

Geographic distribution: Hawks are found worldwide except in Antarctica.

Environment: Hawks live in most habitats, from mountains to coastal regions, grasslands, woodland, and agricultural areas.

Physical description: Hawks are small to medium-sized diurnal birds of prey with sharp, hooked beaks. Hawks are generally brown or gray with lighter barring on the wings and/or back. The red-tailed hawk measures approximately 22 inches long, with a wingspan of about 48 inches and a weight of about 3 pounds.

Interesting facts: The hawk is a highly intelligent bird of prey frequently used for hunting. The female is often bigger than the male. Falcons and hawks are often interchangeable in mythology and folklore.

Myths, folklore, and cultural associations: The hawk is generally recognized in story and myth for its strong wings, piercing eyesight, and reputation for ferocity. Its use as a hunting bird associated it with nobility and aristocracy. In Greek mythology, a hawk served as Apollo's messenger. The collective noun for a group of hawks is a *cast* or a *kettle*.
(See also Falcon.)

Omens and divinatory meaning: Seeing a hawk reminds us of the wild part of our natures. Have you become too immersed in an artificial environment or disconnected from the wilder elements of your personality? Try going for a hike or visit a local arboretum. The hawk can remind you that reconnecting with nature can help balance your life.

Like the falcon and eagle, the hawk can also send the message that something at hand requires your attention, or that you're just not seeing something. Take another look; you may have missed something on your first examination of the situation. The hawk may be recommending that you step back to get a better view of the entire situation; you may be too close to see what's really going on.

Associated energies: Solar symbol, health, sharp sight, protection, strength, perception, observation

Associated seasons: Spring, summer, fall

Element associations: Fire, air

Color associations: Gray, brown, beige

Heron

Name: Great blue heron

Species: *Ardea herodias*

Popular and common variants/subspecies/other names: Great white heron, bittern, spoonbill

Geographic distribution: Heron species are found worldwide except in Antarctica. Many species are migratory. The great blue heron, the most common species in North America, is found in southeast Canada, all of the United States, and Central America. The great white heron, the white equivalent of the great blue, is found in southern Florida, the Caribbean, and the Yucatán Peninsula.

Environment: The great blue heron is mainly found in coastal areas and by inland lakes.

Physical description: The heron is a large, thin bird with a long, narrow neck that can be pulled back into an S shape. The legs are delicate with four-toed feet, three pointing forward and one back. Herons look similar to egrets but are bigger. The great blue heron measures approximately 46 inches long, has a wingspan of about 70 inches, and weighs roughly 5 pounds.

Interesting facts: The heron uses its feet to stir up mud to uncover various mud dwellers to eat, or it uses its feet as lures to attract fish. It also hunts by standing motionless in the water, watching for movement under the surface, before striking with its long, thin beak. The heron is carnivorous. Male and female herons are similar in appearance and share parenting duties. Their courtship and mating are leisurely and relaxed, unlike that of many other birds, and herons often nest in colonies. The collective noun for a group of herons is a *siege*.

Myths, folklore, and cultural associations: One of the folk names for the heron is "henshaw." When Hamlet said he could still tell a hawk from a handsaw (a corruption of "henshaw"), he meant he could distinguish between a hawk and a heron, two birds that were said to be enemies.

Indian folklore says that a heron landing on your house is a sign of good fortune.

One of Aesop's fables tells of a heron that strolled next to a river in shadow, watching for food. It passed up several small fish and ended up going hungry when the sun slowly shifted, and the fish moved to cooler water, out of the heron's reach. The moral indicates that waiting for something better may put you in a position where you end up with nothing.

(See Egret, Ibis, Stork.)

Omens and divinatory meaning: Seeing a heron can be a message to be patient and to choose the correct moment. Stand, watch, and ambush when your moment arrives. On the other hand, waiting too long, like the heron in Aesop's fable, means you can miss your opportunity.

The heron wades through water, stirring up silt and mud to find food. Sometimes you have to stir up some dirt in order to get information to rise. The heron may also be telling you to do some legwork in order to turn something up. Things don't just come your way; you need to get out there and put in the basic effort to lay the groundwork for future success.

Associated energies: Patience, self-reliance, observation, focus, concentration

Associated season: Summer

Element associations: Air, water

Color associations: Gray, white, blue, black, brown

Hummingbird

Order: Apodiformes

Family: Trochilidae

Popular and common variants/subspecies/other names: Ruby-throated hummingbird, bumblebee hummingbird, Anna's hummingbird, rufous hummingbird

Geographic distribution: Hummingbirds are native to the Americas. You'll find hummingbirds from southern Canada all the way down through the United States and Central and South America. Most Canadian and northern United States hummingbirds migrate south for the winter, and some species in Central America may migrate southward as well. Species in warmer tropical areas tend to be year-round residents.

Environment: Hummingbirds are found in meadows, fields, and gardens.

Physical description: Hummingbirds are among the smallest birds in the world, ranging from 3 to 5 inches in length and weighing only a fraction of an ounce. The beak is long and thin.

Interesting facts: Hummingbirds are seemingly miraculous birds; they are the only birds who can fly backward and hover in place for extended periods of time. Conversely, although they can perch, they cannot walk or hop as most other birds do.

Hummingbirds have a reputation for ferocity and will fight one another. They also demonstrate their bravery by flying 500 miles across the Gulf of Mexico when migrating. They are among the fastest birds in the world, able to reach speeds up to 34 mph (54 km/h).

Hummingbirds have the highest metabolic rate of almost any warm-blooded creature, and they must eat almost constantly to fuel their basic functions.

The bumblebee hummingbird is the smallest bird in the world, at approximately 2.5 inches long.

Myths, folklore, and cultural associations: The English name *hummingbird* comes from the hum created by the rapid speed at which the bird's wings flap. John James Audubon called hummingbirds "glittering fragments of rainbows," and they have also been called flying jewels. The sheer beauty of the hummingbird is inspirational.

Urban legend tells of hummingbirds hitching migratory rides on the backs of larger birds such as geese, for it was believed that something so tiny could not possibly fly so far on its own.

A Mayan legend tells that the Creator, after making all the other birds, had a pile of small colorful scraps left over and fashioned a tiny bird out of them. Being made of leftovers is hardly a handicap, however. The Aztecs honored the hummingbird as a symbol of vitality and energy. The Aztec hummingbird god Huitzilopochitli was associated with war and the sun, and the Aztecs believed that warriors would be reincarnated as hummingbirds. Dead hummingbirds were carried as talismans for good fortune in war or to enhance a warrior's battle skill.

In Central America, the hummingbird is seen as a symbol of sexual energy and, by extension, a symbol of love and attraction. In the American Southwest, the hummingbird was associated with bringing rain and much-needed water. The form of the hummingbird was sometimes used as a decoration on water jars, and the hummingbird is a part of ceremonial rain dances in both the Hopi and Zuni tribes, symbolized by a dancer dressed as a hummingbird who dances to summon rain for the crops.

Trinidad and Tobago calls itself "the land of the hummingbird." The hummingbird is featured on the country's coat of arms and the penny; it is also the mascot of Caribbean Airlines.

Omens and divinatory meaning: If you see a hummingbird, chances are good that the message is somehow connected with vitality. The hummingbird may be telling you to watch your energy and not squander it. Although a hummingbird has plenty of vitality, it is carefully apportioned for survival. The hummingbird does not have time or energy to play; it is focused on its basic needs.

What are your basic needs? Are you dividing your energy and attention among too many things, as enjoyable as they may be? Take stock of your commitments and your extracurricular activities, and prioritize them. Make sure to prioritize those things that encourage relaxation and renewal, as well as work and family-related responsibilities.

In addition to warning you to watch how you spend your energy, the hummingbird reminds you to take joy in the simple things, to literally slow down and smell the flowers. Bury your nose in a branch of a flowering shrub or walk among the paths of a public garden to refresh yourself. You need to feed your emotional and spiritual self as well as your physical being. The hummingbird, with its love of bright, sweet things and its colorful, iridescent plumage, gently scolds you to nourish that side of yourself as well, and to embrace joy.

The frequency with which the hummingbird must eat also reminds you to take plenty of small breaks to restore and maintain your energy. Ignoring your basic needs is self-destructive in the long run.

The hummingbird's message can be summed up as urging you to live life to the fullest within your means; don't hold back. Give it your all, but remember to relax and sip the sweetness along the way. Make sure to balance all your commitments in order to best apportion your energy.

Associated energies: Joy, energy, energy management, sweetness, vitality

Associated season: Summer

Element association: Air

Color associations: Green, red, white

Ibis

Name: White-faced ibis

Species: *Plegadis chihi*

Popular and common variants/subspecies/other names: White ibis, scarlet ibis, glossy ibis

Geographic distribution: Ibis are found worldwide. The white-faced ibis, the most common species in North America, is found in the central and western United States, down through Central America, and into the southern part of South America.

Environment: The ibis is found in coastal regions as well as swamps, marshes, and wetlands. Although they are wading birds, many species prefer to roost in trees.

Physical description: The ibis is a wading bird with a long, narrow neck and head and a downward-curving thick beak measuring an average of 26 inches long. The ibis shares visual similarities with the heron, but the ibis's beak is curved, whereas the heron's is straight. The white-faced ibis has dark feathers with a burgundy sheen and a white mask around the eye area. It measures roughly 20 inches long and weighs approximately a pound.

Interesting facts: There are about twenty-six different species of ibis in the world, the smallest being the dwarf olive ibis, which measures only a couple of inches in length. The ibis has a mainly carnivorous diet, eating small amphibious creatures as well as fish and large insects.

Myths, folklore, and cultural associations: Folklore says the ibis is the last bird to take shelter before a hurricane strikes, and the first to emerge once the danger has passed.

The ibis was a sacred bird in ancient Egypt. The ibis family name, Threskiornithidae, is Greek for "sacred bird." The Egyptian god of knowledge and writing, Thoth, is portrayed as having the head of an ibis.

The American stork is sometimes called a wood ibis, as settlers confused the New World herons and storks with the Old World ibis.

The giant ibis is the national bird of Cambodia.

(See also Egret, Heron, Stork.)

Omens and divinatory meaning: Because the ibis is connected to knowledge and writing, seeing this bird can mean that you need to address the process of learning in your life. Have you been struggling with your methods of learning? Try something different. If you're usually an active learner who absorbs information well through hands-on learning, try a visual-based learning style or a verbal style.

Did you abandon your studies at some time? Perhaps it's time to go back to school. If you can't attend full-time, then perhaps take a course here or there to refresh your skills, or catch up on new information available in your career field.

Associated energies: Wisdom, knowledge, communication via writing, connection to the sacred

Associated seasons: Spring, summer

Element associations: Water, air

Color associations: White, black, red

Kestrel

Name: American kestrel

Species: *Falco sparverius*

Popular and common variants/subspecies/other names: Common kestrel, greater kestrel

Geographic distribution: The kestrel is found worldwide. The American kestrel is found throughout North America, Central America, and most of South America.

Environment: Kestrels often prefer open and semi-open environments such as deserts, grasslands, and meadows. They are at home in both urban and suburban regions.

Physical description: A small bird, the American kestrel measures approximately 7.5 inches long, with a wingspan of approximately 22 inches, and weighs about 4 ounces. The kestrel has colorful plumage, including blue-grays, black, rust, buff, and browns in various places. The American kestrel has long, narrow, pointed wings and eye-like spots on the nape of the neck, possibly to mislead potential attackers.

Interesting facts: The kestrel is a subsection of the falcon family, generally recognized by its hunting behavior. It hovers between 30 and 60 feet in the air before diving down to seize prey. In general, kestrels do not build their own nests; they often use the nests of other species.

Myths, folklore, and cultural associations: The kestrel has the folk name of windhover, appropriate because a slight headwind helps the bird hover in place.

It has also been popularly called a sparrowhawk, due to the common belief that it eats small birds such as sparrows, though it is not properly a hawk at all. Although the kestrel does on occasion eat smaller birds, its diet consists mainly of insects and small mammals such as mice.

Historically, the kestrel's ringing, rattling call led to these birds being used as guards for dovecotes, to scare away predator birds.

The common kestrel is the national bird of Belgium.

(See also Falcon.)

Omens and divinatory meaning: The eye-like spots on the kestrel's nape bring to mind the saying "eyes in the back of one's head," and this bird may alert you to watch your back. The kestrel's habit of sitting in high places to survey activity below can also be a signal to step back and take the long view of events or situations. The hovering behavior can signal you to exercise patience and judge your time of action carefully for maximum success and effect.

The kestrel is a small bird but still a predator. Don't discount your own power if you consider yourself smaller in stature or position in some way, be it physical or in an area such as career.

Associated energies: Watchfulness, power in small packages

Associated seasons: Summer, fall

Element association: Air

Color associations: Black, buff, blue-gray, white, rust, brown

Kingfisher

Name: Belted kingfisher

Species: *Megaceryle alcyon*

Popular and common variants/subspecies/other names: Eurasian kingfisher, kookaburra, halcyon

Geographic distribution: Most kingfisher species are found in the Old World, but the belted kingfisher is found throughout North and Central America.

Environment: The belted kingfisher lives near bodies of water such as rivers, streams, ponds, and lakes.

Physical description: A small bird with a long pointed beak, the belted kingfisher has a slate-blue head with a crest, a slate-blue back, a white front, and a white collar around its neck. The female has additional rust-colored markings along her chest and sides and is more brightly colored than the male.

Interesting facts: The kingfisher nests in tunnels or burrows in riverbanks. It hunts by perching, watching the water for prey. When it spots its next meal, the kingfisher plunges headfirst into the water after it.

Myths, folklore, and cultural associations: In general, the kingfisher is seen as a symbol of protection and a good luck charm. Legend has it that the Old World kingfisher had more muted colors than the belted kingfisher of the Americas. Supposedly the belted kingfisher received its beautifully colored plumage when it was the first bird that Noah released from the ark after the floodwaters were confirmed to have receded, and therefore was the only bird to catch the final rays of the setting sun on its breast and the blue of the twilight sky on its back.

One family of the kingfisher suborder is named Halcyonidae, derived from the same root as the English word *halcyon*, meaning idyllic, peaceful, or nostalgic. Greek mythology gives us the story of Alcyone, the daughter of Aeolus (king of the winds), who drowned herself in grief when she discovered that her husband had drowned. The gods rewarded her devotion by turning her into a kingfisher, and Aeolus forbade the winds to blow during the halcyon days (the seven days before and after the winter solstice) so that the kingfisher could lay its eggs. The fabled "halcyon bird" was said to build its nest on the water itself, something that could only be done during the halcyon days when the seas were calm.

In old Europe, carrying a kingfisher feather was thought to provide protection from misfortune. Hanging a dead kingfisher by a string was thought to serve as a wind indicator, as the bird's beak was said to point in the direction from which the wind would come.

Omens and divinatory meaning: Sighting a kingfisher is, in general, a lucky thing. Noting which way the kingfisher was facing may be valuable, as this may be the direction from which good news or an opportunity will come to you.

The kingfisher may bear the message for you to be the one who calms troubled waters, as the legendary halcyon bird was said to do. The halcyon is also said to have possessed the ability to calm winds—you may be the one with the power to clear up muddled communication that's dogging a particular situation in your life.

The halcyon connection may also be a message to evoke some wonderful memories of your past in order to enrich the present.

Associated energies: Precision, timing, good fortune, peace, calm

Associated season: Summer

Element associations: Air, water

Color associations: Gray, blue, white, rust, green, red

Lark

Name: Horned lark

Species: *Eremophila alpestris*

Popular and common variants/subspecies/other names: Crested lark, horned lark

Geographic distribution: Larks are found worldwide, with the largest number of species located in Africa. The horned lark is found from northern Canada down to the southern United States and Mexico.

Environment: This bird favors grassy, open plains.

Physical description: The horned lark is a small brown bird with a buff chest, a black mask, and a black patch surrounded by pale yellow on its throat. This bird has two small feather crests on either side of the top of its head, giving rise to its name. Larks are small to medium-sized birds, about 8 inches in length, with a wingspan of approximately 12.5 inches. They weigh about 1.5 ounces.

Interesting facts: The lark may be best known for its glorious, elaborate song and dazzling aerial displays. Although it flies to dizzying heights, the lark nests on or very near the ground.

Myths, folklore, and cultural associations: Folklore tells us that the lark sings and flies as close to heaven as possible to demonstrate its joy at being alive, something we evoke when we say that someone is "as happy as a lark." The collective noun for a group of larks is an *exultation*, a beautiful reminder of the joy associated with the bird.

Larks were once considered game birds, and they were eaten as part of luxurious feasts. The cheery French-Canadian folksong "Alouette" is about plucking a lark, a fact that astonishes many people when the words are translated for them.

A *lark* is a term for a playful romp or fun activity, often perceived as irresponsible in some way. The word *lark* is also used to describe a person who functions best when he rises early in the morning and goes to bed early.

The Colorado state bird is the prairie lark bunting, which is actually a member of the sparrow family. The meadowlark, the state bird of Kansas, is not a true lark either; it belongs to the *Sturnella* genus, which also includes some blackbirds.

Omens and divinatory meaning: If you see a lark, it could be telling you to cast off the shackles of responsibility for a bit and go on a figurative lark. Play hooky; visit the zoo, the aquarium, or the museum. Get some ice cream or treat yourself to a new book and a full-fat latte. Do something out of the ordinary, something you've always wanted to do but felt wasn't dignified enough, or something you couldn't possibly do because you were too grown-up.

The lark can also be telling you to experience more joy in your life. Are you working so hard that you've forgotten how to have fun?

Think of the image of the skylark, flying as high as it can while singing in sheer exultation. You can figuratively sing out to celebrate the things you love in your life. The lark may be reminding you that you do, in fact, have things to sing about.

Associated energies: Joy, celebration, playfulness

Associated season: Summer

Element association: Air

Color associations: Brown, beige

Loon

Name: Great northern loon or common loon

Species: *Gavia immer*

Popular and common variants/subspecies/other names: Pacific loon, red-throated loon

Geographic distribution: The great northern loon is found in Canada, Iceland, Greenland, Alaska, and the United States. It winters in the British Isles as well as in parts of Europe.

Environment: The loon is found in lakes and ponds.

Physical description: The loon is an aquatic bird with a black head and neck, a ringed collar of white feathers spotted with black, black-and-white spotted or checkered plumage on the back, and a white belly. The pointed bill, legs, and webbed feet are black, and the loon's eyes are ringed with white or gray. The eyes are red in the summer and gray in winter. The common loon measures about 31 inches long and has a wingspan of approximately 45 inches. This bird weighs about 9 pounds.

Interesting facts: Loons are impressive swimmers and divers but are awkward when maneuvering on land because their legs are set far back on their bodies. Consequently, loons find it difficult to take off from the ground and generally must gain speed on top of the water in order to lift into the air, seeming to "run" on the water's surface. To help digestion, loons eat gravel scooped up from the bottom of lakes and rivers.

Myths, folklore, and cultural associations: The word *loon* may come from the Swedish word *lom*, which means "lame," an appropriate description of the loon's hampered mobility on the ground.

If someone is "as crazy as a loon" he is a loose cannon or a wild card. In English the word *loon* sounds like it's related to the terms *lunatic* and *loony*, all words for someone who is deranged or crazy, although *lunatic* and *loony* are derived from the French word *lune* meaning "moon."

The loon has a haunting call that some say sounds like a yodel or a gurgling laugh, but most think of it as a melancholy sound. It is most frequently heard at night.

In a Native American myth Loon and Raven, who were both originally white birds, decided to tattoo one another with designs. Loon was tattooed first by Raven, but when it came time for Loon to tattoo Raven, Raven would not sit still. His restless fidgeting resulted in Loon covering him entirely with the tattoo ink. As Loon fled the scene, Raven threw an oil lamp at him, hitting him in the legs and moving them farther back on his body.

The common loon is the state bird of Minnesota and the provincial bird of Ontario, Canada. It is featured on the back of the Canadian one-dollar coin, which is commonly referred to as a "loonie."

Omens and divinatory meaning: The loon's call is associated with both peace and tranquility. As the loon is a water bird, and water is the element associated with the subconscious and the dream world, hearing or seeing a loon can remind you to pay attention to your dreams. The loon's cry is most often heard after the sun sets, associating the loon with the night, the moon, and with hidden secrets. The night can also be a time of inspiration and creativity as sourced from the unconscious or dream realms.

The loon may also be urging you to let loose and be just a bit crazy for a while.

Associated energies: Dreams, peace, tranquility

Associated season: Summer

Element associations: Water, air

Color associations: Black, white

Magpie

Name: Black-billed magpie

Species: *Pica hudsonia*

Popular and common variants/subspecies/other names: Common magpie (European magpie), yellow-billed magpie

Geographic distribution: Magpies are found in temperate regions of Asia, Europe, and western North America, as well as China and India. The Australian magpie is unrelated to the other species of magpie.

Environment: These birds are found in open woodland, meadows, and grasslands. Magpies are very comfortable in residential areas and around people.

Physical description: A striking bird, the magpie has the deep, glossy black plumage of a crow or raven, with a white chest and white blazes across the top of the wings. The primary flight feathers also have white on them, as can be seen when the magpie flies. It measures approximately 20 inches long (almost half of which is the magpie's long tail), has a wingspan of approximately 23 inches, and weighs about 6 ounces.

Interesting facts: The magpie is believed to be among the smartest of animals. Its chattering call is one of its identifying traits, and, like other corvids, it is a very social bird. The magpie can take more than a month to build a nest due to its size, complex structure, and domed shape. The magpie will also land on larger mammals such as deer to eat ticks.

Myths, folklore, and cultural associations: In China and Korea, the magpie is said to be a bird of good luck and happiness. If a chattering magpie is observed, it means guests will arrive or other good news is on the way. If you hear a magpie when you're setting out, your errand will be blessed with good luck. However, in Western symbolism, the magpie is more often considered a thief or a wastrel and a symbol of bad luck, much like crows and ravens. In England it is considered unlucky to see a single magpie, and to offset the bad luck you must take off your hat and make the sign of the cross or cross two sticks on the ground.

Magpies are attracted to shiny objects and will often filch pieces of tin foil, glossy ribbons, and small coins to hoard. This has given rise to the casual terms "magpie syndrome" or "magpie mind," which describe people being drawn to shiny, pretty things or ideas that distract them from what they should be properly focusing on.

In some American folklore, if a magpie lands on the roof of a house, it is a sign that the house is sturdy and will not collapse or be destroyed in a storm. In other folklore, a magpie landing on the roof or flying past a window means the imminent death of one of the inhabitants.

A commonly known folk rhyme lists the symbolism associated with the number of magpies seen. It is also applied to other corvids such as crows and ravens and has a few different regional variations. Here is one of the most common versions:

One for sorrow, two for mirth,
Three for a wedding, four for a birth,
Five for silver, six for gold,
Seven for a secret not to be told.
Eight for heaven, nine for hell,
And ten for the devil's own self.

In Greek mythology, the nine daughters of King Pierus of Emathia (Macedonia) challenged the Muses to a singing contest. When the sisters lost, they were punished by the Muses for their presumption by being transformed into nine chattering magpies.

A Chinese festival called the Night of Sevens or the Magpie Festival is celebrated on the seventh day of the seventh lunar month. It is a celebration for lovers, something like the Western Valentine's Day. At this time of year the stars Vega and Altair are high in the sky, and in the story these stars represent two lovers, a princess and a cowherd, who were separated forever by the Milky Way. On this festival, all the magpies in the world, out of pity for the lovers' separation, rise up into the sky and form a bridge with their wings so the lovers may spend one night together.

Omens and divinatory meaning: The magpie may be telling you to look for the shiny things around you, to enjoy the bright attractive things in your life. Alternatively, it may recommend that you look at how you balance your love of shiny things with the more serious things in life. Are you too often distracted by the glittery things in life? The magpie can also represent destructive habits; too much hoarding, gossip, idle chatter, or loud talk can harm you or others. But the magpie's black-and-white coloring makes it a symbol of balance, and seeing it can remind you to maintain balance in your life.

Associated energies: Hoarding, distraction, communication, balance between extremes

Associated seasons: Spring, summer

Element association: Air

Color associations: Black, white

Mockingbird

Name: Northern mockingbird

Species: *Mimus polyglottos*

Popular and common variants/subspecies/other names: Blue-and-white mockingbird, brown-backed mockingbird, blue mockingbird

Geographic distribution: Mockingbirds are found throughout southeastern Canada, all of the United States, and the upper part of Central America.

Environment: This bird prefers open ground, parks, cultivated areas, and residential areas.

Physical description: A medium-sized songbird with a long tail, the mockingbird has gray-brown feathers (darker on the back, paler on the chest and belly) with two white bars on the shoulder that become large white flashes when the bird spreads its wings. The mockingbird measures approximately 9 inches long, with a wingspan of 13 inches and a weight of 1.75 ounces.

Interesting facts: Mockingbirds mimic the songs and calls of numerous other birds and continually learn new sounds to imitate. They often sing at night as well as in the daytime. The mockingbird has a large repertoire of mimicked sounds, including machinery and car alarms, and it improvises a great deal, selecting snippets from its existing repertoire and making up new songs as well. It is a cocky and confident bird that is rarely intimidated by larger birds or animals.

Myths, folklore, and cultural associations: The mockingbird is one of the more popular US state birds, being the chosen symbol of five states: Arkansas, Florida, Mississippi, Tennessee, and Texas.

The species name *polyglottos*, meaning "many-tongued," is a reference to the mockingbird's ability to mimic the calls of other birds. Native American names for the mockingbird included "four hundred tongues" and "bird that speaks a foreign language." It is said that the Cherokee used to feed their children mockingbird hearts to help them learn to talk. The English name comes from the word *mock*, an imitation of something. The word *mock* can also mean "to taunt, to jeer at, or to make fun of something," no doubt derived from the mockingbird's mimicry.

Mockingbirds were once very popular caged birds, trapped for pets. This practice is recalled in the lullaby "Hush Little Baby," the first verse of which recounts how "Papa's gonna buy you a mockingbird." The most famous use of the mockingbird in literature is as a central symbol of innocence in Harper Lee's novel *To Kill a Mockingbird*.

Folklore has it that if a mockingbird flies over the head of a single woman, she will be married within the year.

Omens and divinatory meaning: The mockingbird tells you to focus on your communication. Are you using original thought and phrasing, or are you relying on the words of others? Are you hiding behind the opinions of others, even if you have different ideas? Be brave, use your own version, and take your stand.

The mockingbird may also be encouraging you to laugh at yourself. Is it taunting you for ideas or opinions you hold or for an activity you're engaging in? The mockingbird may be reminding you to not take yourself so seriously, to lighten up, and to relax a bit.

The mockingbird can also offer a message of reflection. You reflect your environment (mental, emotional, physical, and otherwise), and your environment also reflects you, although that can be harder to see. The mockingbird reflects the sounds heard in its environment too. If you observe a mockingbird, take some time to examine how you reflect your environment, in both constructive and perhaps unhealthy ways, and use your results to make positive changes in your life.

Finally, the mockingbird may be encouraging you to improvise. Take the ideas or thoughts of others and use them as a starting point for your own ideas and conclusions.

Associated energies: Reflection, communication, humor, improvisation

Associated seasons: Spring, fall

Element association: Air

Color associations: Brown, gray, white

Nighthawk

Name: Common nighthawk

Species: *Chordeiles minor*

Popular and common variants/subspecies/other names: Goatsucker, swisher, nightjar

Geographic distribution: The nighthawk is found throughout Canada, the United States, Central America, and all but the lower third of South America. Nightjars are found worldwide except in New Zealand.

Environment: The nighthawk is commonly found in grassland.

Physical description: The nighthawk has a large head with a small but wide bill made for catching insects. The plumage is a speckled combination of browns, blacks, and whites, which is an excellent camouflage among foliage, shrubs, and leaves on the ground. The nighthawk measures approximately 10 inches long, with a wingspan of about 12 inches and a weight of about 3 ounces.

Interesting facts: The nighthawk, as its name suggests, is a nocturnal bird. It has an impressive flight display at dusk: it will swoop down, then flex its wingtips to change direction and sharply swoop upward again. This flex and shift creates a booming sound. The nighthawk does not build a nest; it lays its eggs directly on the ground. When the nighthawk perches, it often perches lengthwise on its branch or perch instead of across it as other birds do.

Myths, folklore, and cultural associations: The nighthawk isn't a member of the hawk family, nor is it related to them. Nor does it actually suck the milk from goats, as its alternative name *goatsucker* suggests; rather, it eats the insects stirred up by animals.

In Patagonia, the nighthawk's cry was an omen of illness and death. The booming noise made by the nighthawk's wings led it to be associated with thunder and coming rain.

The term *nighthawk* is sometimes applied to a person who remains awake and productive at night, contrary to the lark-like activity of a person who wakes early and is most productive in the morning.

(See also Whip-Poor-Will.)

Omens and divinatory meaning: The nighthawk is most active at dusk, a liminal time between two more clearly defined times. Like dawn, dusk is a magical time, neither day nor night, a time of transition and mystery when anything might happen. A sighting of a nighthawk can foretell the arrival of a time of transition, or it can tell you to take advantage of a transition in which you currently find yourself.

The nighthawk's erratic flight suggests its agility and ability to change direction when necessary. The message associated with this is to remain adaptable and flexible in your life, to not become too used to doing things one way. Pay attention to what is going on around you and be ready to switch direction at a moment's notice to take advantage of something positive or useful.

Associated energies: Adaptability, agility, liminal states, transition

Associated season: Fall

Element associations: Air, earth

Color associations: Black, brown, white

Nuthatch

Name: Red-breasted nuthatch

Species: *Sitta canadensis*

Popular and common variants/subspecies/other names: White-breasted nuthatch, Eurasian nuthatch, brown-headed nuthatch

Geographic distribution: The nuthatch is found throughout the Northern Hemisphere, with the majority of species located in Southern Asia.

Environment: The nuthatch enjoys mature woodland and generally prefers coniferous trees to deciduous.

Physical description: The red-breasted nuthatch is a small, stocky bird with a white face, a buff or rusty breast, bluish-gray back, dark crown and flashes across its eyes, and dark feathers in the wings. The tail and neck are short and the head is comparatively large with a long dark bill. The red-breasted nuthatch measures just over 4 inches long, with a wingspan of approximately 7.5 inches and a weight of about half an ounce.

Interesting facts: The nuthatch walks along trunks and branches with its head downward, probing cracks of bark for insects. It will often move in a zigzag pattern to search for food, hang upside down, or rest and tilt its head to the side to survey its surroundings. The nuthatch will cache food to eat throughout winter.

Myths, folklore, and cultural associations: The nuthatch gets its name from its action of taking a seed or nut, wedging it into a small space or crevice, and hammering at it with its bill.

In his *History of Animals*, Aristotle wrote that the nuthatch and the wren were at war with the eagle, and the nuthatch broke the eagle's eggs, making it a special target for revenge. However, like many other classic stories, there is no real-life association for this fable; eagles don't single out nuthatches for particular attention in any way.

Omens and divinatory meaning: This bird may be encouraging you to take a different view of your situation. The nuthatch's habit of walking down tree trunks and tilting its head to look at things suggests that you should look at things in a different way to gain a better understanding. It may also mean that you courageously go into a new situation headfirst, while still scanning back and forth to be cautious.

The nuthatch may also carry a message to stock up against upcoming lean times. Do you maintain a savings account, into which you put a tiny bit aside every time you get your paycheck? Even if you think you can't afford five dollars a month, make the commitment to hoard even that small amount. Money builds up, and the time may come when you can use the small bit you have put aside to buy necessities in desperate times.

Associated energies: Adaptability, new viewpoints, preparing for the future

Associated season: Summer

Element association: Air

Color associations: Blue-gray, white, black, buff, chestnut

Oriole

Name: Baltimore oriole

Species: *Icterus galbula*

Popular and common variants/subspecies/other names:
Audubon's oriole, golden oriole

Geographic distribution: The Old World oriole family (Oriolidae)
is found across Africa, Europe, Asia, and Australia. New World orioles
(Icteridae) that live in southern Canada and the northern United
States migrate all the way to Central America, a difficult migration
that can claim the lives of younger orioles.

Environment: Orioles are arboreal, meaning they live mostly within treed areas.

Physical description: Orioles have black, yellow, and orange plumage; the female is duller than the male. The bird measures approximately 7 to 9 inches long, has a wingspan of approximately 10 inches, and weighs about 1.25 ounces. The oriole has a long slender beak and tail.

Interesting facts: There are two kinds of orioles, known as the New World oriole and the Old World oriole. They are two different species and, in fact, come from two entirely different families. The New World oriole was likely so named by settlers for its similarity to the familiar Old World oriole.

Orioles build a sort of woven cup- or pouch-like nest that is suspended from a branch. They will generally stay with a partner throughout the breeding season and raise between one and three clutches per year. The oriole is part of the blackbird family.

Myths, folklore, and cultural associations: In China, the oriole represents music and joy; admired for its song, the bird became a symbol of beautiful music. In Chinese, the written word for oriole is composed of the symbols for "beautiful" and "bird." During the Ming dynasty, the oriole was the badge of certain civil officials; it later became the emblem of court musicians.

The Baltimore oriole became the state bird of Maryland in 1947; it was protected by the state as early as 1882 by a specially passed law. The Baltimore oriole was so named because its colors (black and orange-red) are like those of the coat of arms belonging to Lord Baltimore. The oriole is the mascot of Baltimore's professional baseball team, the Baltimore Orioles, and it is sometimes referred to as a golden robin. A Native American creation myth has the oriole, along with the mockingbird, selected as the king of the birds.

In Vainakh mythology, the goddess Seelasat, whose name means *oriole*, is a defender of virgins.

In Poland, if you hear a golden oriole calling, rain is imminent.

An American folk story collected by Florence Holbrook says the oriole was once a hornet, changed into a beautiful bird as thanks for defending the kingdom of the south from a northern attack. This is why the oriole's nest is shaped somewhat like a hornet's.

Omens and divinatory meaning: If you see an oriole, positive change is coming your way. If you have been having emotional difficulty, particularly lack of joy, the oriole reminds you that happiness is in the simple things of life if you only pause to see them, and that often those simple things are already in your possession. The oriole can represent a new creative venture or the imminent awakening of a dormant creative ability.

The oriole's woven hanging nest associates it with handicrafts and creativity. If you see an oriole, examine your current level of creativity. This does not mean solely artistic output, although that can certainly be an element. How do you employ creativity in your life? Do you use creative solutions in your career or workplace instead of relying on the same old basic problem-solving strategies? The oriole encourages you to think outside the box, to access your creative ability and activity, and to experiment.

The oriole also connotes domesticity. If you see one, it may be reminding you to look to your home in order to ensure that it's serving your needs properly. A home should offer a sense of security, relaxation, and safety. It should nurture your spirit and offer you a space for recreation as well as a place where you may rest and recuperate. Your home also provides a space in which you and your family can grow, share, and develop. The oriole reminds you to take time to appreciate your home, to do any little jobs that have been waiting for completion, to tidy up, and to generally take pride in your space.

Associated energies: Beginning of summer, new projects, creativity, sunshine, happiness and cheer, domesticity, positive energy

Associated season: Summer

Element associations: Air, fire

Color associations: Yellow, orange, black

Osprey

Species: *Pandion haliaetus*

Popular and common variants/subspecies/other names: Sea hawk, fish hawk

Geographic distribution: The osprey is found worldwide except in Antarctica.

Environment: The osprey lives along coasts and rivers and near bodies of water in forests.

Physical description: The osprey is a bird of prey that weighs approximately 3.5 pounds, measures approximately 24 inches long, and has a wingspan averaging 5 feet. Its plumage is glossy brown to black on the back, white sometimes streaked with brown on the chest, and white underneath. The osprey's tail is short, the wings are long and pointed, and the dark bill is the classic sharply hooked raptor shape.

Interesting facts: The osprey builds its nest on the top of man-made structures such as telephone poles and buoys, and reuses its nest year after year. The osprey's main diet is fish, which it catches by diving into the water feet first. In order to catch fish more efficiently the osprey has developed small barbs on the undersides of its feet.

Myths, folklore, and cultural associations: Greek mythology tells us that King Nisos of Megara was transformed into an osprey to attack his daughter after she fell in love with Minos, king of Crete.

According to Pliny the Elder's *Natural History*, ospreys made their young fly as close to the sun as they could as a test of their strength and courage, and killed any that failed. English folklore says that seeing an osprey is good luck, but to only hear its scream is bad luck. It was also believed that if an osprey was shot along a coast, the fish would disappear.

Bolivian hunters believed that if they inserted osprey bones under their skin, they, too, would become efficient, successful hunters like the osprey.

An old European folk belief held that fish were naturally so overcome by this bird of prey that they surrendered to it by rolling over in the water so that the osprey could just pick them up, a suggestion that the osprey demonstrated the natural order of things. Another European folk belief said that ospreys had two different feet, one taloned for catching fish and the other webbed for swimming.

The osprey is the provincial bird of Canada's Nova Scotia. Although sometimes called a sea eagle, the osprey is not related to the eagle family in any way.

Omens and divinatory meaning: The osprey, like other raptors, offers the message of perception and acute vision. Its success in abundantly providing for itself and its family also brings a favorable omen for your own success and state of abundance.

The osprey can encourage you to jump into something feet first. Don't overdeliberate an issue; observe, make your decision, and jump! Be certain of your goal, have confidence, and trust yourself.

Associated energies: Perception, abundance, success

Associated seasons: Summer, fall

Element associations: Water, air

Color associations: Brown, white

Owl

Family: Strigidae; Tytonidae

Popular and common variants/subspecies/other names: Barn owl, great horned owl, screech owl, snowy owl, saw-whet owl, barred owl

Geographic distribution: Owls can be found in all geographic regions except in Antarctica.

Environment: The preferred environment depends on the species of owl. Owls can be found in deep forest, deserts, open grassland, and even mountainous regions.

Physical description: Such a wide variety of owls exists that it is hard to provide accurate measurements. Sizes range from the tiny elf owl at approximately 5 inches to the eagle owl at about 28 inches long. In general, owls have two forward-facing facial disks of feathers. The eyes are set in the center of these disks, which can be adjusted to direct light and sound to the eyes and ear holes. Plumage is generally designed to allow these birds to easily camouflage themselves in shadows and foliage.

Interesting facts: Owls are generally nocturnal birds, though some are active at twilight and around dawn as well. Many owls can fly almost silently thanks to special feathers along the edges of their wings. Owls are farsighted and see very well at night. They also have excellent hearing, which enables them to locate prey easily. These birds swallow prey whole or in chunks and regurgitate nondigestible elements, such as bones and fur, in the form of pellets. As their eyes face forward, owls have the ability to turn their heads from side to side over 200 degrees to change their line of sight.

Myths, folklore, and cultural associations: Owls have a complex body of folklore attached to them. In many cultures, to see or hear an owl was an omen of death or ill fortune. In some cultures the owl is associated with sorcery and malicious witchcraft. The negative or fear-filled associations may arise from the fact that owls are active at night, a time when humans are less confident and feel insecure. However, in ancient Greece, owls were associated with Athena, the goddess of wisdom, and were considered lucky. Because Athena was also the goddess of war, the owl was considered a lucky omen for soldiers. The association with the owl crosses to Athena's Roman cognate, Minerva, as well. An owl also accompanies (or carries) Lakshmi, the Hindu goddess of prosperity and wisdom.

In ancient Rome, a dead owl nailed to the door of a home protected it from evil. The Romans associated the owl with shapeshifting witches. In various Native American tribes, the owl could be a sign of impending ill luck, illness, or death. However, in Wales, the owl's cry was said to be a harbinger of the loss of virginity, which isn't necessarily a negative.

In ancient Egypt, the owl hieroglyph represented the letter M and symbolized wisdom, mystical goddess-related knowledge, and secrets, all associations still commonly made with the owl today. We call people who are active and productive at night "night owls." The collective noun for a group of owls is a *parliament*.

Omens and divinatory meaning: The owl, with its ability to see and hear very precisely, can cut through obfuscation and murk. It may be bringing you the message that you have the ability to do the same if you focus. The owl cannot see anything up close, so it may be warning you to pay closer attention to things around you. Don't be blind to what's happening right under your nose.

Many of the owl's cultural associations are negative, but look beyond that for a moment and see the owl as a messenger from the darkness and uncertainty of life, from the Otherworld, or from your subconscious. Instead of fearing it for its news, appreciate and welcome it. You may be loath to receive news that is not positive or in your favor, but having advance notice is actually a valuable thing, because you can prepare for a challenge or difficulty.

The owl may be reminding you to access your own wisdom and intuition, to see through illusion or deception, or to trust yourself in a time of uncertainty.

Associated energies: Keen sight, excellent hearing, wisdom, prophecy

Associated season: Fall

Element association: Air

Color associations: Brown, buff, white, gray

Parakeet

Name: Budgerigar, budgie

Species: *Melopsittacus undulatus*

Popular and common variants/subspecies/other names: Shell parrot, Australian budgerigar, zebra parrot

Geographic distribution: The parakeet, properly called the budgerigar, is naturally found in Australia, South America, Africa, and Asia. Flocks of feral budgerigars have developed in cities located in non-native areas.

Environment: The budgerigar is found in grassland, open woodland, and scrubland.

Physical description: The name *parakeet* is applied to any number of small parrots, but in North America it tends to refer to the budgerigar, colloquially termed the budgie. It is a small bird with a thick neck and long tail, generally with green, yellow, and black plumage, although breeders have diversified the coloring to include white, blue, violet, and other colors. In the wild, the budgerigar measures approximately 7 inches long with a weight of approximately 1.25 ounces. Birds bred in captivity are usually larger.

Interesting facts: The budgerigar is one of the most popular pet birds in North America. The parakeet will preen flock mates and feed them via regurgitation.

Myths, folklore, and cultural associations: A small parrot, the parakeet carries many of the cultural associations that parrots in general do. General folklore has it that if parrots whistle, rain is coming, and that it is unlucky to kill a parrot. Old American folklore suggests that if a young woman likes parrots, she will become an old maid.

Known for its mimicry, the parakeet can be trained to imitate sounds, songs, and words. It is a playful bird and enjoys toys and tricks. Because of their ability to learn to talk, parrots are often associated with communication. Parrots are often perceived as birds that sound intelligent, but in reality they say little of original substance—we say someone is "parroting" something if she simply repeats it without thought or reflection.

Omens and divinatory meaning: The parakeet is often associated with simplicity and pleasure. Its ability to mimic connects it to reflection. If you see a parakeet, it may be bringing you the message to examine yourself and your actions for original behavior. Are you simply reflecting what's going on around you? Are you regurgitating other people's opinions instead of thinking things through for yourself?

As a popular cage bird, the parakeet may also be reminding you to look at your current situation. Are you feeling caged in some way? Are you restricted or unable to spread your wings and fly as you would truly like to? If the answer is yes, then you need to think about how you can change things. A caged creature is wholly dependent on others for safety and welfare; the parakeet may be telling you to be more independent. The parakeet may also be suggesting that someone else considers you a pet instead of a serious friend or partner.

Associated energies: Play, reflection, captivity

Associated season: Summer

Element association: Air

Color associations: Yellow, green, white, blue

Partridge

Name: Gray partridge

Species: *Perdix perdix*

Popular and common variants/subspecies/other names: Hungarian partridge, English partridge

Geographic distribution: The partridge is found in southern Canada, the northern United States, Europe, Asia, Africa, and the Middle East.

Environment: The partridge prefers flat land such as fields, meadows, and cropland.

Physical description: The partridge is a small chicken-like bird approximately 12 inches long with a wingspan of approximately 21.5 inches and weighing approximately 16 ounces. This bird has a short neck and tail and short rounded wings. Its plumage is gray and brown on the back and wings, with a white or off-white belly. Most males and some females have a brown horseshoe-shaped mark on the chest.

Interesting facts: The partridge lays an average of fifteen eggs in a single clutch. It both nests and feeds on the ground.

Myths, folklore, and cultural associations: Real partridges are not native to North America; they were imported from Asia and Europe, where they have served as game birds from ancient times to the modern day.

The species name *perdix* comes from a Greek myth. Daedalus, the famous architect and designer of such places as the Labyrinth of Crete, threw his nephew, Perdix, off a roof in jealousy because the nephew's talent and skill threatened to surpass Daedalus's own. Athena saved Perdix from death by changing him into a bird as he fell. The partridge, therefore, stays close to the ground and does not roost in high places such as trees. The partridge is also associated with Venus, the Roman goddess of love, which may explain the gift of a partridge in a pear tree given in the traditional Christmas song. Christian interpretations of the song theorize that the partridge represents Christ and the pear tree the cross of crucifixion.

In one of Aesop's fables, a partridge was added to a farmer's flock of chickens. The chickens pecked at it, and the partridge took himself off to be alone, thinking they were picking on him because he was different from them. Then he observed the flock bickering and pecking at one another. The partridge stopped feeling sorry for himself when he realized that the chickens were just as willing to mistreat one another as they were to mistreat him. The moral of this story demonstrates that there is no point in complaining about strangers' bad behavior toward an outsider when those strangers behave badly toward one another as well.

(See also Grouse, Quail.)

Omens and divinatory meaning: The partridge's large clutch of eggs makes it a symbol of fertility. It may be telling you that the time is ripe for expanding or developing new ideas or projects. The partridge's association with Venus also makes it a romantic symbol, so the message may be specifically directed toward physical fertility or romantic opportunity. Remember, fertility doesn't necessarily mean physical reproduction or giving life; it can also mean a time rich or ripe for whatever you have planned, or an abundance of something.

The partridge's plumage and ability to blend into the ground also make it a symbol of stealth and staying out of sight. This bird may be warning you to operate quietly for a while, not making too big a splash in order to accomplish your goals.

Associated energies: Fertility, camouflage, abundance

Associated seasons: Fall, winter

Element associations: Earth, air

Color associations: Brown, white, gray

Pelican

Name: American white pelican

Species: *Pelecanus erythrorhynchos*

Popular and common variants/subspecies/other names: Brown pelican

Geographic distribution: Species of pelicans are found on all continents except Antarctica. The American white pelican is found in central Canada, the central and western United States, and Mexico.

Environment: Pelicans live by inland and coastal bodies of water.

Physical description: Large water birds with long, pouched bills, pelicans measure an average of 60 inches long; the beak alone measures approximately 12 inches. A pelican's wingspan averages about 105 inches, and the birds weigh an average of 15.5 pounds. These birds have short legs and tails, and webbed feet.

Interesting facts: Pelicans live in colonies and are social birds. In fact, white pelicans often fish in groups, cooperating by herding a school of fish into one area and then catching their food together. The pelican scoops water and its prey up together in its bill but must drain the throat pouch before swallowing the fish. The American white pelican catches its food while swimming, but some other pelican species dive for fish.

Myths, folklore, and cultural associations: Pelican hatchlings were once thought to wound their mother's breast then drink blood from it, possibly a misunderstanding of the chick's action of throwing itself against the pouch to push the food up past the mother's bill. This led to the Christian use of the pelican as a symbol of atonement and self-sacrifice. Folklore once said that pelicans killed their young, then brought them back to life with the blood fed to them, and thus the pelican was also used as a symbol of resurrection. The pelican can also stand as a symbol of Christ, whom Christians believe shed his blood and sacrificed himself to redeem humankind, and was then resurrected. Due to their tendency to nest in colonies, pelicans have been considered symbols of good parenting.

The pelican was representative of the fourth of the five stages of alchemy, an ancient science of transmutation of basic elements into gold and to discover the secret of eternal life (an allegory of refining the self and spirit to attain perfection). Again, it is the legend of piercing its own breast to feed its young that sources this association. In the fourth stage of the alchemical process, the practitioner must delve inward to forge a connection with his own soul and spiritual energy, figuratively breaking himself open in order to allow the newly refined spiritual self to emerge.

Because of these associations, the pelican is connected more broadly with spiritual growth and devotion in general than with earthly matters.

Omens and divinatory meaning: The pelican reminds you of many things, among them the need to give selflessly to others. Have you been miserly lately? Have you been jealously hoarding your time, your energy, or your resources when people around you desperately need them? The pelican teaches you that sharing can enrich you instead of making you the poorer for your actions.

The pelican also encourages you to examine your parenting style. Are you giving too much of yourself? Not giving enough? Symbolically sacrificing yourself for your children also denies you your right to have a life of your own. On the other hand, withholding too much from children can deprive them of the structure and support they need to grow. Balance is the key to a strong, healthy relationship between parent and child. If you do not have children, look at your relationships with your pets or close friends.

Associated energies: Devotion, self-sacrifice, charity, strong parenting

Associated seasons: Spring, summer, fall

Element associations: Air, water

Color associations: White, brown, black, yellow

Petrel

Name: Fork-tailed storm petrel

Species: *Oceanodroma furcate*

Popular and common variants/subspecies/other names:
Shearwater, snow petrel, fulmar, Bermuda petrel

Geographic distribution: The petrel is found off the Pacific Coast in the northern United States, Canada, and Alaska, as well as in Europe.

Environment: A seabird, the petrel lives along coasts, spending most of its time at sea.

Physical description: The storm petrel is a small gray to bluish-gray seabird with a swallow-like silhouette. It measures approximately 8 inches long, with a wingspan averaging 17 inches, and weighs about 2 ounces.

Interesting facts: Storm petrels are pelagic, meaning they only return to land to breed, where they nest in colonies. They spend the majority of their time in the air or on the water. They feed by hovering just above the water, often with their feet touching it, giving the impression that they are standing or walking on the water's surface. Chicks are not fed in bad weather; if the chick's metabolism isn't maintained, it slips into torpor and ceases growth until the weather clears up and the parent returns to revive it with body warmth and food.

Myths, folklore, and cultural associations: The name *petrel* is said to derive from the name of Saint Peter, who managed to walk on water when he saw Jesus doing so, although Peter sank when his faith wavered. The petrel presents the illusion of walking on water when it flies just above the surface, looking for food.

A petrel seen close to shore is often interpreted as a sign of bad weather coming, as the bird is thought to have been blown inland. Petrels will sometimes follow ships in the approach of a storm in order to shelter in the lee of the ship, the side protected from the wind.

Storm petrels were once called Mother Carey's chickens. Mother Carey is a folkloric figure whose name may be a corruption of *Madre cara*, "dear mother," a prayer to the Virgin Mary. The Bermuda petrel, known as a cahow, is the national bird of Bermuda.

Omens and divinatory meaning: The chick's ability to go torpid and put growth on hold until bad weather clears is significant. The petrel may be advising you to pull back and hibernate for a bit until storms have passed, at which time you can resume your activity. The petrel may also be warning you of approaching bad weather, either literal or figurative.

The petrel can be encouraging you to have faith in yourself and your abilities. Don't doubt yourself, or you may start to sink. Have faith in what you're doing.

Associated energies: Energy conservation, faith

Associated seasons: All seasons

Element associations: Air, water

Color associations: Gray, blue-gray, white

Pigeon

Name: Rock pigeon (feral pigeon)

Species: *Columba livia*

Popular and common variants/subspecies/other names: Domestic pigeon (*Columba livia domestica*)

Geographic distribution: Pigeons are found in Southern Canada, all of the United States, Central America, South America, as well as most of Europe, parts of Africa, the Mediterranean, coastal Asia, and parts of Australia.

Environment: Pigeons dwell in cities and urban areas, as well as in agricultural regions.

Physical description: A plump bird with a small head, short legs, and blue-gray plumage, the pigeon measures approximately 12 inches long, with a wingspan of 22 inches and a weight of about 11 ounces.

Interesting facts: For the pigeon, breeding is dependent on an abundant food supply. In the wild, this may be once a year, but in cities pigeons can breed year round. Pigeons travel in close flocks for safety; a lone pigeon is generally an unsafe one.

Myths, folklore, and cultural associations: The pigeon may be the world's oldest domesticated bird, appearing in both ancient Mesopotamian and Egyptian records. Pigeons belong to the same family as doves but have very different cultural associations. Whereas doves are perceived as blessed or pure, pigeons are often perceived as dirty pests.

Pigeons have an excellent navigational ability and have frequently been employed for communication in various situations. Julius Caesar used them, as did the Arabs during the Crusades. In World War II, certain pigeons even received decorations for bravery. Pigeon racing, a challenge in which domesticated birds (sometimes referred to as carrier pigeons or homing pigeons) are released to find their way home and the winner is the one who accomplishes this within the least amount of time, has been (and still is) a popular sport.

(See also Dove.)

Omens and divinatory meaning: The pigeon is a determined creature. It will stay in an area as long as there is food, despite attempts by humans or other birds to chase it away. The pigeon sighting can encourage you to be stubborn and hang in there, regardless of what challenges are thrown in your path. The pigeon also has strong connections to house and home. If a pigeon appears to you, take a look at your relationship with your home. What does it represent to you? What would you like it to be for you? If these things don't match up, you know you have work to do. The pigeon is safest in a flock. Don't discount the strength and support found in a community. Furthermore, remember the importance of communication within that community; don't assume people know things just because you do. Make sure everyone is in the loop regarding important information.

Associated energies: Community, cooperation, communication

Associated seasons: All seasons

Element association: Air

Color associations: Gray, blue, white, buff, brown

Plover

Name: American golden plover

Species: *Pluvialis dominica*

Popular and common variants/subspecies/other names: Piping plover, black-bellied plover, mountain plover, lapwing, peewit, killdeer

Geographic distribution: Plovers are found worldwide except in polar regions and the Sahara Desert.

Environment: The plover is generally considered a shorebird, but the golden plover is also found in grassland such as prairies, mudflats, tundra, beaches, and other open ground.

Physical description: A medium-sized shorebird, the plover measures approximately 10 inches in length, with a wingspan of 22 inches and a weight of about 5.5 ounces. Plumage is speckled gold and brown on the back, with a black chest and belly and a white rump. The plover's face is black with a white border; the bill and legs are black.

Interesting facts: The plover runs in starts and stops, looking for food along the ground. It has excellent eyesight that enables it to see tiny insects. The plover commonly employs the "injured parent" ruse: it will run back and forth, faking injury in front of a predator to draw danger away from the nest and chicks. The American plover has a very long migratory route, from northern Canada and Alaska to southern South America, much of which takes place over water where it cannot land to eat or drink.

Myths, folklore, and cultural associations: At one time golden plovers were believed to contain the souls of those people who assisted at the Crucifixion and therefore were doomed to wander forever for their sin against Christ. This may refer to the bird's migratory habits or to its behavior of running in starts and stops.

An English folk belief has it that to see seven plovers together was an omen of misfortune. Folklore tells us that if you hear a plover call in the morning, someone you know will soon die. To see a plover was also considered a sign of upcoming rain.

In Hawaiian mythology the golden plover is a bird form of the legendary figure Kumukahi, related to the deity Pele, who was a healer said to enable people to perform miracles. In Iceland the golden plover is a sign of summer.

Omens and divinatory meaning: The plover's long migratory route indicates that it must prepare well in advance for the journey or die along the way. The plover can teach you about long-range planning and encourage you to look beyond the short term in order to prepare for maximum efficiency.

The plover's start-and-stop search for food and its keen eyesight suggest that you keep an eye on the details. Thoroughly cover short stretches of ground at a time, instead of wandering aimlessly.

Associated energies: Preparation, advance planning, travel

Associated season: Summer

Element associations: Air, water

Color associations: Black, white

Puffin

Family: Alcidae

Genus: *Fratercula*

Popular and common variants/subspecies/other names: Atlantic puffin, tufted puffin, horned puffin

Geographic distribution: The Atlantic puffin is primarily found along northern coasts of the Atlantic Ocean, with the majority in Iceland. Tufted and horned puffins are found along the northern coasts of the Pacific Ocean. All species winter farther south along their respective coasts.

Environment: The puffin lives at sea and breeds in rocky sea cliffs on coasts or islands.

Physical description: The puffin is a stocky, chubby bird with a large head and short blunt wings. It has a large triangular bill that is colored bright red, blue, and yellow in the summer breeding season; the bright colors dull significantly afterward as the colored plates on the beak are shed. The puffin has short legs with orange webbed feet; white cheeks, chest, and belly; and a black head and back. The tufted puffin has a black belly and yellow feathery tufts that sweep back over the head from above each eye. Puffins average 14 inches in length, with a 23-inch wingspan, and weigh approximately 1.5 pounds.

Interesting facts: The puffin is a pelagic seabird, meaning it spends little time on land. Puffins nest in colonies on rocky cliffs or sometimes in burrows. Both parents feed the infant puffling until it is very fat, then leave the chick, which must make its own way to the sea. Like penguins, the puffin is comically awkward on land but spry and agile in the water. Its short flipper-like wings help it dive and seem to "fly" through the water. The puffin can use its wings to fly, although it must flap them rapidly. However, it is ungainly in the air and cannot travel for long distances this way.

Myths, folklore, and cultural associations: Irish folklore tells that puffins are reincarnations of monks. This association is reflected in the genus name *Fratercula*, meaning "little brother."

One of the common nicknames for a puffin was "sea parrot," due to its colorful beak.

Puffins were once hunted for their meat, eggs, and hide, and puffin meat is still eaten in Iceland. However, in the Middle Ages people could not ascertain whether puffins were birds or fish, and because they could not be safely classified, eating them was forbidden.

In Yorkshire, England, puffins were associated with witches and witchcraft. As puffins are gregarious birds, to see one alone is usually considered unlucky. To avert this misfortune, regional superstitions variously advocated killing a lone bird, throwing a stone at it, making the sign of the cross, or removing an item of clothing and putting it back on inside-out or backward.

Some versions of the Arthurian legend say that at the end of his life, King Arthur was transformed into the form of a puffin instead of a crow or raven.

The Atlantic puffin is the provincial bird of Newfoundland and Labrador in Canada.

Omens and divinatory meaning: The puffin is often laughed at for its clownish appearance and ungainly maneuvering outside the water. Seeing one may remind you to be cheerfully true to yourself, no matter what people say about you. Remember, too, that everyone has his strengths. You may not be a master of landing or taking off, but no one can touch you when you're in your home element.

If you're a parent or a caregiver, the puffin may be telling you that it's time to back off and let your chick make its own way to the sea.

> **Associated energies:** Parenting, being true to yourself, playing to your strengths
>
> **Associated season:** Summer
>
> **Element associations:** Water, air
>
> **Color associations:** Black, white, orange, yellow, blue

Quail

Name: Northern bobwhite quail

Species: *Colinus virginianus*

Popular and common variants/subspecies/other names: California quail, mountain quail (note: the illustration depicts a California quail)

Geographic distribution: Various species of quail are found across the United States, southern Canada, and Mexico. The northern bobwhite is found in the eastern United States. Species of quail are found worldwide, including arctic zones.

Environment: Quail generally prefer open woodland and brushland.

Physical description: Quail are small rotund birds and generally have short necks, wings, legs, and tails. Many have a characteristic curved or angled plume on top of the head. Quail measure approximately 11 inches long, have a wingspan of approximately 15 inches, and weigh an average of 7.5 ounces.

Interesting facts: Quail can fly, although they are weak fliers and prefer to walk or run on the ground; their bodies are designed for the latter. They lay large clutches of eggs and often travel in small groups, eating or resting together while one or two keep watch for danger.

Myths, folklore, and cultural associations: The Old World quail belong to the pheasant family (Phasianidae). The New World quail are a different family (Odontophoridae), named for their visual similarity to the Old World birds.

Quail are common game birds, hunted for food. They are also associated with lust and intimacy, and in fact the term *quail* at various times was a pseudonym for prostitute. Quail have a somewhat frenzied, active courtship and mating process, which may serve as inspiration for the association.

We use the term *quail* to mean to draw back in fear or to cower from something.

The quail is associated with such deities as Artemis and Apollo, because Hera turned their mother Leto into a quail out of jealousy. The quail is also connected with Hercules, who was once brought back to life by the scent of a quail roasted by his companion Iolaus.

German farmers used to catch quail and keep them in cages inside the house as protection against lightning. The quail was also sometimes used as a symbol representing Russian tsars. In ancient Rome, quail were kept as fighting birds and were thus associated with courage. Folklore has it that if you hear a quail call within two weeks of naming a baby, you have chosen the correct name for it. The California quail is the state bird of California.

Omens and divinatory meaning: The quail's large clutches of eggs associate this little bird with fertility and fecundity. The quail may be telling you that the time is ripe for a new project or endeavor. The quail is also successful at escaping and hiding from pursuit or danger. This bird can bring you the message to keep your head down, to remain invisible until a threat has passed. Alternatively, if a quail reveals itself to you, it may be giving you the message that things are quiet enough that it is safe to come out, that whatever threats you have been dealing with have now passed.

The quail will often burst out of hiding while being chased, engaging in a short frenzied burst of flight to escape danger. Therefore, a quail may be advising you to invest an extra burst of energy to complete a project by a deadline, or to wrap up a particular era in your life that is slowing down the rest of your positive evolution or development.

Associated energies: Caution, fertility, fecundity, courage, tenacity, nourishment

Associated seasons: Fall, winter

Element associations: Earth, air

Color associations: Brown, black, white, gray, blue-gray

Raven

Name: Common raven

Species: *Corvus corax*

Popular and common variants/subspecies/other names: Chihuahuan raven

Geographic distribution: Ravens are found worldwide, in a variety of climates.

Environment: Ravens prefer wooded areas with open spaces nearby, mountainous regions, coastal areas, and rural areas, although some can be found in cities or other human settlements.

Physical description: The common raven averages 25 inches in length, has a wingspan of approximately 54 inches, and weighs 2.6 pounds. The plumage is a glossy black. Ravens typically live between 10 to 15 years in the wild. The raven's beak is large and heavy, and has a slight curve to it. The feathers around the beak are slightly shaggy or downy, and the tail is wedge shaped. The raven has a distinctive croaking call.

Interesting facts: Ravens are very sociable birds that mate for life. The raven has a comparatively large brain for its body size and has demonstrated remarkable intelligence and problem-solving abilities. Ravens are capable of mimicking a wide range of sounds, and, like crows, ravens play both with others of their species and with other creatures. They also trick other species into doing some of their work for them. For example, if there is an animal corpse they wish to dine on, they will call or lead a larger animal to the site to open the corpse, enabling the raven—an omnivore—to access the inside. Like their relatives the crows, ravens are carrion scavengers, but they also eat insects, small animals, and fruit and grains. Ravens from cooler climates have larger bills than ravens in warmer climates.

(See also Crow.)

Myths, folklore, and cultural associations: The collective noun for a group of ravens is an *unkindness*, suggesting their association with unpleasantness. Like crows, their black plumage; harsh, unattractive cry; and propensity for eating carrion also mark ravens as birds of ill omen. Noah is said to have first released a raven from the ark in hopes that it would return with proof that the floodwaters were receding, but the raven did not come back. The superficial reading of this story is that the raven didn't care enough to return or failed in its assigned task, but the underlying implication is that the raven may indeed have found land and went on to live its own life. Swedish folklore holds that ravens are spirits of the dead. German mythology further refines that to ravens being specifically damned souls.

Despite the mainly negative associations of the raven, many Native American tribes and clans honored this bird as a creator and/or a trickster figure. In both cases, the raven's intelligence is one of its defining characteristics.

Possibly the raven's ability to mimic human speech has caused it to appear as a messenger, prophet, or other communicator of supernatural knowledge in myths from a variety of cultures. Odin of Norse myth had two raven companions, Huginn (thought) and Muninn (memory).

British legend has it that England will never fall to an invader so long as there are ravens in residence at the Tower of London. One theory is that Charles II put them there in response to a fortune-teller's advice that disaster would befall England if they were ever to leave it. The belief that the ravens have been there without break is erroneous, however; they were reintroduced after World War II, and the Tower now maintains ravens with clipped wings so they cannot fly away.

One of Aesop's fables tells of a raven who saw a swan and desired its beautiful plumage for its own. Reasoning that the swan's coloring and beauty must come from its habitat, the raven forsook its usual environment and bathed in ponds and rivers. But no matter how hard he scrubbed he could not change the glossy black of his feathers to the brilliant white of the swan's, although he tried day after day. He eventually died from starvation, because he could not feed himself in this new habitat. The moral of the story is to be true to your own nature and to follow your true path instead of trying to create change by implementing someone else's methods. The raven teaches you to trust yourself and your chosen way.

The English word *raven* may come from the Norse word *hrafen*, meaning "to clear one's throat," a reference to the raven's harsh croak or coughing cry.

The common raven is the official bird of Canada's Yukon territory.

Omens and divinatory meaning: Ravens, like crows, tell you to remember to enjoy life while you shape it and travel through the stormy seas of change. Remember to laugh at yourself when you make a mistake; find the joy in everyday things. Like most corvids, ravens are attracted to shiny, sparkly things when they are young. Bring some physically shiny, pretty things into your living space and metaphorical ones into your life to brighten it, and remind yourself to appreciate the beauty around you. Allow yourself to indulge in small luxuries now and again; it's good for your morale and for your soul.

Ravens are also associated with the occult, meaning hidden knowledge and secrets, and are linked with magic and prophecy. If you are interested in working with the occult and the Otherworld, the raven may be a good companion. Likewise, the raven may be a good guide if you are preparing for an introspective journey to get to know yourself better or if you feel that you have lost your sense of self-identity. The raven's black feathers can represent the unconscious; do not fear it, but rather value it for the fertile possibilities it holds.

The raven can also be a symbol of patience. In many myths, the raven is portrayed as a trickster who carries out long, elaborate plans to achieve his goals. In a myth from North America's Pacific Northwest, the raven desires the sun, which is being held jealously by a chieftain in a lodge. The raven turns himself into a pine needle, which is swallowed by the chieftain's daughter. The daughter then births the raven as a son, and when he grows he asks to play with the sun as a ball. When it is given to the boy the raven escapes with the sun and returns it to the sky, restoring light and warmth to the world. The raven can remind you to be patient and farsighted; some plans take longer to come to fruition than others. The same goes for some of the practical jokes the raven has played in Native American myth. Genius cannot be rushed.

Associated energies: Insight, being true to oneself, play, appreciation of luxury, prophecy, death

Associated season: Winter

Element associations: Air, earth

Color associations: Black, blue, purple

Robin

Name: American robin

Species: *Turdus migratorius*

Popular and common variants/subspecies/other names:
European robin (*Erithacus rubecula*)

Geographic distribution: The American robin is found throughout North America, from as far north as Alaska and Canada and south through Florida and Mexico. Although some robins remain in southern Canada or the northern United States, most migrate in late summer or early fall to winter along the coast of the Gulf of Mexico. They return north in late February or early March. European robins are found throughout Europe, with related subspecies found in Eurasia and northern Africa.

Environment: Robins are found in woodland, agricultural, and urban areas. The robin is comfortable in residential areas and with human company.

Physical description: The American robin is approximately 10.5 inches long, with a wingspan averaging 13 inches, and weighs approximately 2.5 ounces. The back feathers are brown, the throat area is white with black specks, and the stomach and underside of the tail are also white. The robin's chest area is red or reddish orange. The European robin resembles a sparrow or bluebird, with a brown back, a grayish front, and a reddish-orange patch beginning on its face and extending down over the top of its chest.

Interesting facts: American and European robins are not from the same family. American robins are thrushes of the Turdidae family that will flock and migrate. The smaller European robin (*Erithacus rubecula*) is from the Muscicapidae family and is related to the flycatcher instead of the thrush. The European robin is mostly nonmigratory, but the robins that live farthest north in Europe do move somewhat southward during the coldest part of the year.

The American robin is diurnal but assembles in larger flock groups at night. The robin is one of the first birds to begin singing at dawn.

The robin is also one of the first birds to begin laying eggs after its return from migration. A robin's eggs are light blue in color, giving rise to the paint/dye hue known as robin's egg blue.

Primarily a ground feeder, the robin hops along the ground after rainstorms or in freshly overturned soil, looking for worms and insects—one of the bird's most familiar behaviors. In winter robins will gather in flocks to eat and spend a lot of time in trees, which makes them harder to spot than during spring and summer.

Myths, folklore, and cultural associations: Much of the lore associated with robins comes from Europe and has been transferred to the American robin. In European tradition, the robin is said to be associated with storms and the Norse god of thunder, Thor. Much of the folklore involving the robin depicts it as a very compassionate bird. In the late sixteenth-century poem "Babes in the Wood," a robin comes across the bodies of dead children and covers them with leaves, mosses, and flowers. Shakespeare also mentioned this bit of folklore earlier, in *Cymbeline*.

Several different legends describe the source of the robin's red breast. One says that the red breast is the result of the robin being burnt by the heat of Hell when the bird descended there to bring back the gift of fire to humanity; an alternate myth states that the robin was scorched when bringing water to the souls in Purgatory. Yet another version has the robin in the stable where Christ was born, watching Mary and her child sleeping. When it saw that the fire was almost out, it fanned the embers with its wings. When the flames revived, they singed the robin's breast, and when the feathers grew back they were the color of flames. Another myth has the robin flying to Christ's shoulder in order to sing and comfort him during the Crucifixion, and being stained by a falling drop of Christ's blood. Alternately, while attempting to pull the crown of thorns off of Christ's head the robin stained its own breast with the blood on the single thorn it succeeded in drawing out.

Despite the robin's association with compassion, good luck, and blessing, if the bird flies into a house it is a sign that a death will soon take place there. If a robin is killed, accidentally or otherwise, ill fortune will come to the one who caused the bird's death.

Perhaps the most popular piece of folklore associated with the robin is that its return presages the coming of spring. Your first sighting of a robin after a long winter is said to be very lucky. (Obviously, this bit of folklore isn't as pertinent if you live in a southern region where the robin has a year-round presence.)

Although the robin is connected with the arrival of spring, it also has a strong association with winter and Christmas, thought to have developed because the postmen of Victorian England, whose visits increased in frequency at Christmas due to the volume of mail, wore red uniforms and were therefore addressed as "Robin." In the pagan myth of the Oak King and the Holly King, archetypes of the light and dark halves of the year, respectively, the Oak King triumphs over the Holly King at the winter solstice and thereby initiates the return of the light to the land. This myth is paralleled in the folk belief that a robin kills a wren at the winter solstice and is crowned king of the waxing year. Folklore has Robin Redbreast as the husband of Jenny Wren, an interesting pairing considering the robin/wren battle.

The robin is the state bird of Connecticut, Michigan, and Wisconsin in the United States. It was also voted the national bird of Britain in the 1960s.

Omens and divinatory meaning: The robin is a welcome harbinger of spring. Likewise, sighting a robin can inform you of something new just around the corner, likely something anticipated or long awaited, or some kind of relief after a long period of work or privation. If you've been waiting to begin a new project, this may be the time to do it.

If you've been feeling at odds with a particular situation in your life, or if things in general have been feeling out of place or out of rhythm, try looking down. Robins hop along newly overturned soil to find food. Examine freshly disturbed situations within your life and seek the nuggets of wisdom, benefit, or positive results that may be there.

The robin also encourages you to step outside. Find cheer in the natural world, in gardens or wild places. Go for a walk in the rain and splash in the puddles. Try adding a dash of bright red to your wardrobe, such as a silk scarf or a pair of socks to cheer you up.

The robin's message can be summed up as: new beginnings are on the way. Watch for opportunity or the seeds of a new venture or project to develop. Joy, happiness, and cheer will be yours.

Associated energies: Cheer, new beginnings, celebration, cycles, compassion, good fortune

Associated season: Spring

Element associations: Air, fire

Color associations: Brown, red

Sandpiper

Order: Charadriiformes

Family: Scolopacidae

Popular and common variants/subspecies/other names: Spotted sandpiper, upland sandpiper, solitary sandpiper, curlew, snipe, woodcock

Geographic distribution: Sandpipers can be found worldwide except in Antarctica and the driest deserts.

Environment: The sandpiper is a shorebird, comfortable along the edge of almost any water source, including oceans, lakes, rivers, marshes, and ponds.

Physical description: Sandpipers characteristically have long legs, necks, and bodies, with narrow bills. Their coloring generally consists mainly of browns, buffs, and whites. Sandpipers range in size depending on the species but are roughly from about 7 inches up to 2 feet long. This bird's average weight ranges between 1 and 8 ounces.

Interesting facts: The sandpiper's typical behavior is to dart back and forth in the edge of the surf on beaches, watching for the foam to retreat so the bird can dip its thin, sensitive bill into the wet sand to find food. Sandpipers are primarily waders; they do not swim often, but they do fly well, and they follow a long migratory path.

Myths, folklore, and cultural associations: The name *sandpiper* refers to the bird's preferred environment of the shore and to the piping call it makes as it rises into the air or senses danger.

Snipes, woodcocks, and curlews are also members of the sandpiper family, and much of their lore is also applicable to sandpipers. Sighting a curlew at sea was a sign of bad weather and associated misfortune, as they are considered shorebirds. Hearing them call at night was an omen of upcoming bad luck. In parts of Scotland the curlew was called "the Judas bird" because its call gave away the hiding place of Covenanters, members of a rebel Scottish Presbyterian movement, to those searching for them.

Omens and divinatory meaning: The sandpiper is a liminal bird, most at ease in the damp area of the shore between the water and the land. It represents balance and ease in moving back and forth between two states of being, able to handle being not fully committed to one or the other. The sandpiper may be telling you that being betwixt and between two situations isn't such a disaster after all. Be comfortable in your position and trust in yourself. Share in the best of both worlds.

The sandpiper's darting movements may also suggest to you that you can make quick forays into new ground. The bird's method of seeking food and feeding may encourage you to look beneath the surface for whatever it is you seek, in order to find what is of value to you.

Associated energies: Scavenging, quickness, balance, willingness to seek below the surface

Associated season: Summer

Element associations: Earth, water, air

Color associations: Buff, beige, brown, white

Sparrow

Name: House sparrow

Species: *Passer domesticus*

Popular and common variants/subspecies/other names: Field sparrow (*Spizella pusilla*), white-throated sparrow (*Zonotrichia albicollis*)

Geographic distribution: Sparrow species can be found in Europe, Asia, the Mediterranean regions, and all across North America.

Environment: The sparrow is closely associated with human habitation, especially agricultural areas. It adapts well to living in human civilization and urban areas. It is less likely to be found in mountainous, tundra-like, or rainforest environments.

Physical description: Sparrows are small, chubby, brown or brown/gray birds with blunt beaks for eating seeds. Males tend to have black or dark brown masks on their faces, whereas females tend to be brown all over. Sparrows measure approximately 6 inches long, with a wingspan of about 8 inches. They typically weigh just under an ounce.

Interesting facts: Pairs of sparrows are typically monogamous and mate for life, although behavior contrary to this exists. However, the male house sparrow's relationship with his nest site—typically found in cavities or holes and hollows—is more important than his relationship with his mate. The sparrow may lose a mate, but he won't relinquish his nest. If a mate is lost it is rapidly replaced. If a bird does not find a mate, it may associate itself with a breeding pair and serve as an assistant. A pair of house sparrows can produce up to four broods in a season.

The sparrow is a very social bird that constantly gathers in groups. It is relatively nonranging; a group may roam over a few miles but will not move beyond that.

The sparrow is the most common songbird in North America and yet is not a native species. The house sparrow was introduced to North America in the mid-1800s to control crop-threatening insects. The sparrow population then exploded, threatening in turn various fruit trees and associated crops by eating them.

Myths, folklore, and cultural associations: There is a tendency to call any small bird a sparrow, meaning that much Old World lore about sparrows may not in fact be specifically associated with a bird of the true sparrow family. This doesn't invalidate the large body of cultural lore associated with sparrows, however.

Sparrows appear in classical poetry and sacred texts as positive birds. The Roman poet Catullus wrote a series of poems about his lover's relationship with her pet sparrow, culminating in a poem of mourning entitled "Lesbia's Sparrow" that outlined her grief at the death of her beloved bird. Sappho's poem "Hymn to Aphrodite" describes the goddess's chariot as being pulled by sparrows (although some translations give the honor to doves instead). This may be an example of the sparrow's subsequent association with love and affection. In the Gospels of Luke and Matthew, Jesus refers to sparrows. In Luke 12:6 he points out that five sparrows may be sold for a mere two pennies, but that does not make them worthless in the eyes of God. In Matthew 10:29 he states that two sparrows may be sold for a single penny, but not a single sparrow falls to the ground without God's knowledge. Both these examples use the sparrow as a demonstration of a small and apparently insignificant part of the natural world that is still recognized as valuable by a Creator.

In his *Ecclesiastical History of the English People* (circa 731 C.E.), the Anglo-Saxon historian and theologian Bede compares the life of man to a sparrow flying through a house in winter: While inside, the sparrow is safe from the winter storm and elements, but once outside again it vanishes into the darkness from which it came. The statement is couched in a discussion about conversion to Christianity, perceived as a comforting philosophy when human life is like the sparrow in the allegory, emerging from the unsure darkness and returning to it again.

The sparrow's omnipresence (again, possibly because the word can refer to any number of small brown birds) also demonstrates the tendency to associate something overly familiar with something vulgar. The sparrow was sometimes used as a symbol for the lower classes in European iconography, as opposed to more noble birds that represented the nobility. That vulgar association also translated to an association with lewdness, possibly also a reference back to the connection with Aphrodite, goddess of love.

That familiarity can be seen in the use of the sparrow in Egyptian hieroglyphs too. The symbol doesn't represent a sound and has no phonetic value; instead, it is a determinative that is paired with words to identify something as small, narrow, or bad.

The Italian sparrow is the national bird of Italy.

Omens and divinatory meaning: The sparrow spends much of its life in flocks and feeding groups. Seeing a sparrow encourages you to look at how you're functioning within your own social group or communities. Are you connecting to people, or are you withdrawing from them? We all need communities for support, companionship, and stimulation in order to grow. Examine your connections and sort out which ones nourish and support the life you want to live. If you realize that you need more support in certain areas, work to redress those imbalances. Likewise, evaluate the relationships you do have. Are they healthy? Is there a balanced exchange of energy, or does one of you draw more from the other on a regular basis? Sometimes you have to be firm and defend your own energy from being absorbed or even abused by others.

The sparrow's connection to its nesting site also invites you to look at your home, your spiritual refuge. Is it in order? Is it tidy, or is it a mishmash of objects that don't have assigned places? Does your home have a temporary feeling to it, as if you're not quite grounded or are expecting something better? Make the best of what you've got. Sort through the jumble of stuff that accumulates, and sell, give away, or donate what you no longer need. Paint the walls; hang pretty curtains; move furniture around to stimulate the energy of your environment. Making a change doesn't have to be an expensive undertaking. Flourish where you are.

The story of the sparrow being important in the eyes of God also counsels you to trust that you are in the place you are supposed to be in and walking the path that was intended for you. Trust that the universe has you in the correct place in order for you to learn, grow, and develop.

Do you feel overlooked or not special? The dullness of the sparrow's appearance and ubiquitous presence in no way reflect its worth. Remember that you are unique, that you have your own value and much to offer the world around you. Celebrate that.

The sparrow's message may be summarized as: Trust yourself and your path. Remember that who you are and what you do are of value. Examine your relationships and your connection to the communities around you, and make sure that your participation in them is healthy.

Associated energies: Companionship, adaptability, union, survival, sharing, value, self-worth

Associated seasons: All seasons

Element associations: Air, earth

Color associations: Brown, gray, black

Starling

Species: *Sturnus vulgaris*

Popular and common variants/subspecies/other names: Mynah

Geographic distribution: Starling species are found throughout Asia, Europe, and Africa, and have been introduced to New Zealand, Hawaii, and North America.

Environment: Starlings can be found in almost any environment worldwide except deserts. They are particularly at ease in urban and suburban areas.

Physical description: Starlings are medium-sized songbirds measuring about 8.5 inches long, with a wingspan of approximately 13 inches and an average weight of 2.5 ounces. They have yellow beaks and black plumage with an iridescent sheen; their feathers dull to brown in winter and develop small white speckles.

Interesting facts: Starlings are strong fliers and are very social birds that flock often. They also make a lot of noise and are often identified by their garrulous chatter. Excellent mimics, they often incorporate sounds from their environment into their calls.

Myths, folklore, and cultural associations: The name *starling* is supposedly taken from the bird's silhouette when flying; the head, tail, and wings look like a star shape from below. The starling is not native to North America; it was introduced from Europe in the late nineteenth century and has flourished.

The starling is a talkative bird, and this is reflected in its collective noun, a *murmuration* of starlings. Mozart owned a starling as a pet and was enchanted by its ability to mimic his musical compositions. The starling is said to have been one of the birds beloved by Druids, and in fact *druid* is the Gaelic term for *starling*.

The mynah is a bird in the starling family. The word *mynah* comes from the Hindi term *maina*, meaning "delightful," and is used as a term of endearment for pets or children. Mynah birds were encouraged to nest in Hindu temples.

Starlings thrive in cities and can become problematic there. So many starlings nested in Big Ben of London and perched on the minute hand that they stopped the clock in 1949.

Omens and divinatory meaning: The starling's gregariousness reminds you to get out and be social. Have you been spending too much time alone? You may need regular contact with other people to counteract the time spent in your head. A change of scenery and a change of company is healthy.

The starling also tells you to communicate, but make sure you're not just contributing to general chatter. Too much talk at the same time obscures what everyone has to say. Make sure that what you say is spoken thoughtfully and clearly, and listen in your turn. Otherwise it's all just noise and a waste of energy and effort.

Associated energies: Community, communication

Associated seasons: Summer, winter

Element association: Air

Color associations: Black, white

Stork

Name: Wood stork

Species: *Mycteria americana*

Popular and common variants/subspecies/other names: White stork (*Ciconia ciconia*)

Geographic distribution: Storks are found worldwide except in Antarctica and parts of Australia. The wood stork is the only stork found in the Americas. It lives on the Atlantic coasts of the southern United States, both the Pacific and Atlantic coasts of Central America, and throughout the upper two-thirds of South America. The white stork is found in Europe, Africa, and Asia.

Environment: The wood stork prefers marshes and swampland.

Physical description: The wood stork has long dark gray legs, a long white-feathered body, and a long thin neck. This bird is roughly 38 inches tall, weighs about 6 pounds, and has a wingspan of approximately 60 inches. The wood stork has a dark, almost bald head and a deep, yellow-brown, downcurved beak that resembles that of an ibis. The trailing edge of the wing, when exposed, is black.

Interesting facts: The stork is essentially mute, as it possesses no syrinx (the avian equivalent of the larynx). Storks tend to communicate in hisses or whistles and with beak chattering. The large wings are the first things stork chicks develop; the legs grow long later. Storks use their wings in a soaring, gliding flight, a style that conserves physical energy by employing thermal air currents.

Myths, folklore, and cultural associations: One of the most common pieces of stork folklore connects the birds with childbirth, perhaps a direct connection to the abundance of European storks that nest on roofs of homes, the folklore coming from a time when home births were the norm. By extension, storks are associated with family. Actual recorded interaction with their own young is less inspirational, however; storks will sometimes kill and consume their chicks.

Storks were sacred to Venus in Roman mythology. It was said that if a stork built a nest on your roof, you were blessed by Venus and would enjoy a love-filled life. Aristotle proposed that killing a stork be made a criminal act. Storks are said to care for their aging parents, and the Romans legislated what was called a "stork law" decreeing that children must care for their elderly parents.

Storks are also said to be the enemy of snakes, which in the Christian tradition associates them with vigilance and holiness because serpents are linked with evil.

The white stork is the national bird of Lithuania, Ukraine, and Poland.

(See also Heron, Ibis.)

Omens and divinatory meaning: The stork is a quiet bird. Seeing one can raise the question of how much you're talking. Perhaps you should experiment with silence for a bit and listen instead of chattering.

The stork's gliding flight encourages you to go with the flow in order to conserve energy. Don't waste energy by fighting to accomplish something; the easiest path is via accepting the flow of things. You can learn more that way, too, by passing through situations you might not otherwise have encountered. Be open to the journey.

The stork can also ask you to look at how you treat various members of your family. Are you favoring some over others? Are you giving all the care they require?

Associated energies: Fidelity, acceptance, family relationships and responsibilities

Associated season: Summer

Element associations: Water, air

Color association: White

Swallow

Family: Hirundinidae

Popular and common variants/subspecies/other names: Barn swallow, bank swallow, purple martin

Geographic distribution: Swallows are found on all continents except Antarctica.

Environment: Swallows prefer open habitats, such as grasslands, meadows, and marshes. Being near water appeals to them.

Physical description: The most identifying physical attribute of a swallow is the long tail, which is sometimes forked and sometimes squared. They have short bills, but strong jaws that open wide. Most swallows are dark blue or green above and pale on their undersides. Swallow species range in length from about 4 to 10 inches, and their weight ranges from about 0.4 to just over 2 ounces.

Interesting facts: In constant motion, the swallow displays a seemingly erratic flight that results from chasing airborne insects.

Myths, folklore, and cultural associations: A legend tells that the Christ child was once playing in the mud, making little bird shapes that came to life as swallows. People once believed that swallows hibernated in mud by or under water during the winter; not until the end of the nineteenth century did ornithologists agree that swallows instead migrated.

The swallow is said to have flown about Christ on the cross, crying, "Cheer up! Cheer up!" In Christian symbolism, the swallow's return each spring represents the Resurrection.

Swallows spied at sea are a good omen, as their presence means land is near. To kill one is bad luck or will cause a rainy season, to step on an egg will render a woman infertile, and to disturb a nest will ruin crops. The swallow is also a symbol of freedom, as it does not survive well in captivity.

The swallow's courage is notable: it will attack humans that come too near its nest, which can be problematic because certain types of swallows like to build nests in house eaves. Folklore decrees that a swallow's nest built on your house is a lucky thing, and the swallow will protect your home from fires or storm damage. On the other hand, a flock of swallows landing on your roof was said to warn of upcoming poverty. A bird in the house is generally considered a bad omen; however, it is said that a swallow in your home brings good luck.

The barn swallow is the national bird of Austria and also of Estonia.

Omens and divinatory meaning: Swallows are well known for their seemingly overnight return in spring. This abrupt return is a sign of hope and renewal. Seeing a swallow tells you that there is a sudden reversal for the good in your future. The swallow's sudden return is also a symbol of rapid change in general. Watch for things to happen quickly in your life.

The abundance of folklore about swallows nesting in or near houses also makes the swallow a symbol of hearth and home. If you sight a swallow, think about what it may be telling you about your home. Do you love your home and identify with it? Is it safe? Does it provide spiritual renewal, or is it just a place to crash when you aren't somewhere else? Take a good look at your home and what it means to you, and take steps to make it as positive a place as you can.

Associated energies: Hope, cycles, renewal, hearth and home, courage

Associated season: Spring

Element association: Air

Color associations: Blue, green, cream, rust, brown

Swan

Genus: *Cygnus*

Popular and common variants/subspecies/other names: Trumpeter swan, whistling swan, mute swan, black swan, whooper swan, tundra swan

Geographic distribution: Swans live in mainly temperate climates. They are found throughout the Northern and Southern Hemispheres with the majority of species in the former. Swans are not found in Central America or tropical Asia.

Environment: Swans live on or near water, feeding both in water and on land.

Physical description: Males and females look alike, although males are generally heavier. The larger species, such as the mute, trumpeter, and whooper swans, can reach lengths of more than 60 inches and weigh more than 33 pounds, with wingspans of almost 10 feet.

Interesting facts: Swans usually mate for life and maintain their pair bonds socially, even in the nonbreeding season. However, "divorce" is not unknown. The name *swan* comes from an Indo-European word meaning "to sing" or "song."

Myths, folklore, and cultural associations: Swans tend to be associated with grace, beauty, magic, and illusion in myth and story. Swan-maiden legends tell of women who shapeshift or who remove their swan skins to bathe in human form. The "Swan Lake" story is a classic example. Likewise, the Celtic tale of Aengus depicts this story. Aengus, the Irish god of love, fell in love with Caer, a girl who appeared to him in his dreams. After searching, he found her along with 149 handmaidens, all cursed to live a year as swans, then a year as human women. Aengus was told he could marry Caer if he could successfully identify her out of the whole flock of swans. When he succeeded, he chose to turn himself into a swan to be with her, and their song as they flew away together put her captors to sleep for three days and nights. Also from Irish mythology comes the legend of the four children of Llyr, who were transformed into swans by their father's second wife, Aoife. They remained swans for nine hundred years until their curse was broken by the prophesied marriage of a chieftain from the north to a woman from the south. When the children of Llyr were transformed back into human shape, however, they were not restored to their youthful forms but rather to aged, decrepit, withered bodies, and they died almost immediately of extreme old age.

Greek mythology tells us of Cycnus, who threw himself into a lake out of grief and was turned into a swan. His name gives us the Latin word for swan, *cygnus*. The Greek god Zeus turned himself into a swan to seduce Leda and father the twins Castor and Pollux. Saraswati, the Hindu goddess of creativity, enlightenment, and the arts among other things, is sometimes depicted as sitting with a swan that symbolizes the ability to discern between the eternal and the transient. In Norse myth, swans were associated with Freya, the goddess of fruitfulness and abundance, rain, and sun. Swans have also been associated with royalty, wealth, and prestige. The swan is also connected with dreams and voyaging between the seen and unseen worlds.

Hans Christian Andersen's popular story called "The Ugly Duckling" tells of a baby waterfowl who looks quite unlike his duckling siblings. He is awkward, and his physical differences make him feel unloved and misunderstood. The end of the story shows that the misfit was not a duckling at all, but a cygnet who grew into a stunning adult specimen whose final form outshines the smaller, duller ducks. Andersen also penned a story called "The Wild Swans" in which a jealous stepmother transforms her eleven (sometimes seven) stepsons into swans. The boys' sister may break the curse, but only if she sews the brothers shirts from cloth woven of thread made of nettles that she has broken down and roughly spun herself, while remaining silent and unspeaking.

The mute swan is the national bird of Denmark, while the whooper swan is the national bird of Finland.

Omens and divinatory meaning: If you see a swan, transformation lies in your future. Do you feel unwanted or unappreciated? Your time to shine is imminent. Are there issues in your life you can alter or transform to yield more positive results and benefits? Perhaps the swan is encouraging you to make physical changes in your life in order to revitalize yourself. Try a new hairstyle, a new food, or rearrange your furniture. Sometimes a change is as good as a rest.

The swan also encourages you to pay more attention to your dreams—they may be trying to tell you something. Try keeping a dream journal by your bed, even if you only jot down a scarcely remembered image or two. Dreams are a symbolic bridge between your subconscious and conscious minds. They are a way for your mind to work out things troubling it and to process events and emotions experienced during the day.

The swan coaxes you to look at your life to discover the magic it holds. It also urges you to pierce any illusions operating in your life at the moment. Sometimes you cannot see what is plain to others; it may be the result of an illusion you cling to in an attempt to protect yourself, or an illusion being projected by others to deceive you. In either case, sweep it away. Truth without illusion may be painful to deal with at first, but in the end it will be better for you and will allow you to grow.

Associated energies: Transformation, grace, beauty, compassion, fidelity, love

Associated season: Summer

Element associations: Water, air

Color associations: White, black

Swift

Family: Apodidae

Popular and common variants/subspecies/other names: Chimney swift, white-throated swift, Vaux's swift, European or common swift (*Apus apus*)

Geographic distribution: Swifts can be found on all continents except Antarctica.

Environment: The swift is found in urban areas and forests.

Physical description: The swift has small spines or spikes extending from the end of its tail. The typical swift has large eyes, a wide mouth for catching insects in the air, and short legs with small feet.

The standard swift has an aerodynamic cigar-shaped body with a crescent-shaped wingspan. The chimney swift measures about 5 inches long, with a wingspan of about 11 inches and a weight of just under an ounce. This bird's plumage is generally dark.

Interesting facts: Once thought to be part of the swallow family, swifts are actually more closely related to hummingbirds. Swifts are among the fastest birds, with recorded speeds ranging between 75 and 100 mph. Swifts can copulate while flying and can remain airborne for long periods—not surprising because they cannot perch well with their small, weak feet. Swifts can even sleep while flying and can cling to vertical surfaces. They can go torpid in bad weather if food is unavailable.

Myths, folklore, and cultural associations: Swifts are often confused with swallows, and the chimney swift is sometimes erroneously referred to as a chimney swallow. Like swallows, their return from migration is a sign of summer. The name reflects their speed in flight.

One of their epithets is "the Devil's bird," possibly due to their rare interaction with humans. Swifts spend most of their time aloft, landing only to build nests and incubate eggs.

(See also Swallow.)

Omens and divinatory meaning: The swift is always moving, always traveling. Seeing one can be an omen of upcoming travel. Alternatively, it can suggest that perhaps you've been spending too much time in motion, and that it's time to rest for a while.

The swift's association with the chimney also relates it to hearth and home. The chimney is a part of the fireplace, a source of heat, light, comfort, and energy for cooking. The chimney also serves as a visual connection between the home and the realm of the gods, rooted in the spiritual heart of the home and drawing the eye upward to the heavens. The swift's preference for such a nesting place suggests communication with the deities. If a swift appears to you, it may be reminding you to be more aware of your relationship with the Divine.

Associated energies: Speed, agility, travel, movement, hearth and home

Associated seasons: Spring, summer

Element association: Air

Color associations: Black, gray, brown

Thrush

Name: Wood thrush

Species: *Hylocichla mustelina*

Popular and common variants/subspecies/other names: Fieldfare, song thrush

Geographic distribution: Thrushes are found worldwide. The wood thrush is found in southeastern Canada, the eastern half of the United States, the eastern coast of Mexico, and Central America. The fieldfare is found in northern Europe and Asia, with migratory time spent in southern Europe, North Africa, and the Middle East. The song thrush is found throughout Eurasia.

Environment: The wood thrush prefers woodland with a thick underlayer of scrub and brush, ideally with water nearby.

Physical description: The wood thrush is a medium-sized thrush, with a brown back and white chest and belly with brown spots. This bird measures approximately 8 inches long, with a wingspan of approximately 12 inches and a weight of 1.5 ounces.

Interesting facts: The male wood thrush is noted for its beautiful song. Its syrinx (the avian voice box) is divided so that it can sing two notes at once. The wood thrush is monogamous during a breeding season. This bird is a member of the thrush family (Turdidae) that also includes the American robin and the common blackbird.

Myths, folklore, and cultural associations: An odd piece of folklore associated with the thrush is that after ten years, it discards its original pair of legs and grows new ones. Another strange belief is that thrushes are actually deaf, and that they can speak several languages. It is said that if a thrush sings at sunset, the next day will be fair. If it builds a nest high in its chosen tree, American folklore has it that something bad will happen in the neighborhood.

Hearing a wood thrush sing its beautiful song near your house is said to be very good luck. No doubt the American writer Henry David Thoreau would agree with this. He was much inspired by the thrush and mentioned it several times in his journals. On July 5, 1852, he wrote: "The thrush alone declares the immortal wealth and vigor that is in the forest . . . . Whenever a man hears it, he is young, and Nature is in her spring. Wherever he hears it, it is a new world and a free country, and the gates of heaven are not shut against him . . . . This bird never fails to speak to me out of an ether purer than that I breathe, of immortal beauty and vigor."

In a legend of the Native American Oneida tribe, the Creator decided to gift birds with song and promised the most beautiful song to the one who could fly the highest. The thrush, knowing his small size would be a handicap in the competition, concealed himself in the feathers of the eagle. The birds flew toward the sun, and one by one turned back, exhausted. The eagle flew the highest, then, believing himself the winner, began his return to earth. At that moment the thrush, who had fallen asleep, awoke and began his own flight upward. He passed the eagle's highest point and found a hole in the sky to a wondrous land of great beauty, where he heard a beautiful song. He learned this song and flew back down to earth, where he was met by the disapproval of the other birds for his deception. Ashamed, the thrush hid itself in the thick woods, and this is why the thrush has the most beautiful song but keeps to the forest and is rarely seen. (There is a similar myth about the wren demonstrating cunning by stowing away on the eagle's back in order to be crowned king of the birds; see Wren.)

The wood thrush is the official bird of the US capital city Washington, DC; the rufous-bellied thrush is the national bird of Brazil; and the blue rock thrush is the national bird of Malta.

Omens and divinatory meaning: "Be heard and not seen" could be a phrase applied to the thrush. There are times when what you have to say is more important than having your presence noticed. The thrush can remind you to focus on your words and your message.

A monogamous bird, the thrush is a symbol of commitment. It can also be seen as a symbol of cleverness, for its method in gaining the most beautiful song of all the birds was certainly clever. Its subsequent shame, however, may suggest that you are carrying guilt that perhaps you have taken upon yourself.

Associated energies: Voice, message, beauty, commitment

Associated season: Summer

Element association: Air

Color associations: Brown, white

Turkey

Name: Wild turkey

Species: *Meleagris gallopavo*

Popular and common variants/subspecies/other names: Domestic turkey, ocellated turkey (*Meleagris ocellata*)

Geographic distribution: Native to the Americas, the turkey is found throughout eastern North America, with pockets throughout the western part of the country and Mexico. The ocellated turkey is found in the Yucatán Peninsula.

Environment: The turkey is typically found in open forests, on the ground.

Physical description: The turkey is popularly identified by the red, fleshy neckpiece on its throat (the wattle) and the red, drooping fleshy growth above its beak (the snood). The other common identifier is the fan-shaped tail tipped with brown (domestic turkey tails are tipped with white). In general the turkey's plumage is dark brown to black with white speckles, and the face is blue or gray. The wild turkey's length averages 44 inches, the wingspan averages 4 feet, and the weight averages 10 pounds.

Interesting facts: Domestic turkeys, descended from wild turkeys, usually cannot fly due to their large size, but wild turkeys are perfectly capable of flying.

Myths, folklore, and cultural associations: Folklore says that if you visit a house and a turkey gobbles at you, you are welcome there. If turkeys are sitting in trees and won't descend, snow is on the way.

Ozark Mountain superstition in the United States said that if a girl hid dried wild turkey bones around a room in which she met a young man to whom she was attracted, he would be more amorous. A variation of this belief said that carrying a dried wild turkey wattle with you would draw love into your life. Another common belief says that if two people pull apart a dried turkey wishbone, the one who gets the larger half will have good luck. In a variation of this custom, two people make silent wishes, and the one whose half is larger has her wish granted.

The turkey is sometimes associated with cowardice, because a turkey's (rather sensible) response to danger is to run away. We also call someone who is foolish or irresponsible a turkey, likewise something that is a failure. However, to Native Americans the turkey was considered a spiritual symbol of wisdom. Some tribes wrapped their dead in turkey feather blankets or robes, as they considered turkeys psychopomps (guides to the afterlife) who escorted the spirits of the dead to the afterlife. Turkeys were only hunted if other game was scarce, a fact that bewildered the European settlers when they arrived in North America and saw the turkey as abundant game being apparently ignored.

Early American writer and statesman Benjamin Franklin is said to have proposed the turkey over the eagle as America's symbolic bird, citing its wisdom and intelligence. That's quite the glowing recommendation for a bird that Americans tend to consider as nothing more than food.

Omens and divinatory meaning: Thanks to being the main attraction at the meal for the American holiday of Thanksgiving, the turkey is associated with abundance and plenty. It is a symbol of blessing and a connection to the nourishment that the land can provide for us.

The Native American perception of the turkey as a symbol of wisdom can be applicable to your sighting of the turkey. Are you exercising adequate wisdom in your daily life, or is there something you are deliberately remaining ignorant of in order to keep your life easier? We tend to think of owls as symbols of wisdom, but the turkey demonstrates great wisdom in vanishing when there is trouble. Only a fool remains in a problematic situation and expects to escape unscathed. Wisdom can also help you determine if a particular fight is one you need to stay and win, or one you can step away from for the good of all.

The folk beliefs associating the turkey with romance suggest that it can be linked with a stable family life and a happy home too.

Associated energies: Abundance, gratitude, nourishment, wisdom

Associated season: Fall

Element associations: Earth, air

Color associations: Brown, red, gray

Vulture

Family: Cathartidae

Popular and common variants/subspecies/other names: Condor, turkey buzzard, black vulture

Geographic distribution: New World vultures are found in southern Canada and throughout the United States, Central America, and South America. Old World vultures are found in Europe, Asia, and Africa.

Environment: Vultures are found in open plains and grassland, wooded areas, and deserts.

Physical description: The vulture is a large bird with black or brown plumage, a bare, featherless head, and long wings. The turkey vulture measures approximately 28 inches long, with a wingspan of about 68 inches and a weight of about 4.5 pounds.

Interesting facts: The New World vultures are not the same family as the Old World vultures (or buzzards) but are likely named so for the similarity in physique and behavior. Vultures are carrion eaters, consuming offal and bones or bone marrow; they rely on others to kill prey and on their own excellent sense of smell to locate food. Many vultures have bald heads and/or necks, which makes keeping clean while eating carrion easier. The turkey vulture doesn't have a voice box and thus doesn't have a specific call, but this bird does communicate with hisses or croaks.

Myths, folklore, and cultural associations: Vultures and buzzards are New and Old World versions of the same bird. In Cherokee myth, the turkey vulture (also known as the turkey buzzard) created mountains and valleys by flapping its wings.

The Old Testament of the Bible warns that being eaten by buzzards after death is the worst fate imaginable, but Zoroastrians placed their dead on open towers so as to enable them to be eaten by vultures. The vulture has a cultural association of something that dines on carrion and therefore is lurking in wait for us (or something in our life) to die so that it can feed. Alternatively, vulture feathers have been used as amulets against rheumatism and were believed to be able to bring the dead back to life.

The vulture's association with death links it with ill omens. We say someone is "watching like a vulture" for someone to make an error so that he may swoop in and take advantage of misfortune. These birds haven't always had a negative association, however. The buzzard was one of the birds said to be sacred to Artemis, the Greek goddess of the hunt. In Egypt, buzzards were a symbol of protection and women's health.

Folklore tells us that after the first vulture has been seen in the spring, one may be assured that there will be no more frosts. In the Caribbean, the vulture is sometimes referred to as a carrion crow.

Omens and divinatory meaning: The vulture may be warning you that a person in your life is waiting for you to mess up, ready to feed on the metaphorical corpse of your body, ideals, career, relationships, or just about anything else. This individual may not be actively doing you harm, but he or she is ready to take advantage of your weaknesses.

It can be hard to shake that negative image of the vulture watching for a misstep, but instead of seeing this bird as solely a dark omen, look at your life closely to determine what has been outgrown or is no longer useful. If you are holding on to habits that are no longer supportive (or are outright detrimental), the vulture can help you dispose of them. In this way, the vulture's function is healthy and indeed beneficial to you.

Associated energies: Death, disposal, improvement of health or general state of being

Associated seasons: Fall, winter

Element associations: Air, earth

Color associations: Brown, white, cream, black

Waxwing

Name: Cedar waxwing

Species: *Bombycilla cedrorum*

Popular and common variants/subspecies/other names:
Bohemian waxwing, Japanese waxwing

Geographic distribution: Waxwing species can be found in Eurasia, North America, and northeast Asia. Cedar waxwings are found throughout North and Central America, with the greatest concentration found in southern Canada and the northeast United States.

Environment: These birds are fond of open woodland, fields, grasslands, and suburban areas.

Physical description: Cedar waxwings average 6.5 inches in length, with a wingspan of approximately 10 inches and a weight of about an ounce. This bird's head and chest are pale brown, the belly pale yellow, and the tail is gray with yellow or orange. The face and upper throat are marked with a black mask. One of the cedar waxwing's most identifiable aspects is the small patch of bright red feathers on each wing, resembling drops of red sealing wax. The waxwing also has a crest on top of its head that it raises or lowers.

Interesting facts: Courting waxwings will pass objects back and forth to one another, particularly food. A high-fruit diet means these birds can sometimes become intoxicated or inebriated if the fruit they consume has begun to ferment. They share food sources and dine in flocks.

Myths, folklore, and cultural associations: In the Middle Ages, the waxwing's appearance was an omen of the plague. The red patches on the wings were sometimes said to be drops of hellfire, carrying illness and epidemics. The Dutch name for the waxwing, *pestvogel*, literally translates to "plague bird."

In Germany, it is said that seven years must pass between waves of waxwings returning to the country, possibly connected to the plague patterns of long ago, but more sensibly related to the regular pattern of colder weather forcing the waxwings into parts of Europe they do not habitually frequent in search of food.

In Irish folklore, waxwings are the torchbearers for the banshee, a spirit that wails to alert a family that a relative's death is nigh.

Omens and divinatory meaning: The cedar waxwing that shares food with its flock can appear to remind you to share as well. Are you keeping things to yourself a bit too much? Are you hoarding? Do you know of someone who needs a pick-me-up, and do you have the perfect thing to cheer her? Sharing with someone can increase your joy by observing her pleasure as well.

The waxwing's older associations with plague can also be a warning to mind your health. Have you been eating healthfully? Are you getting enough rest? The waxwing's particular love for berries and fruit can indicate a problem with a sweet tooth. Alternatively, if you've been working too hard, a small treat can be good for you; just don't overdo your reward.

The waxwing's tendency to indulge itself to excess can also be a warning. Are you overindulging in something? Are you partying too hard when you should be reserving your energy to take care of your responsibilities?

Associated energies: Sharing, affection, gluttony, sweet tooth

Associated season: Summer

Element associations: Air, fire

Color associations: Brown, yellow, black, red, orange

Whip-Poor-Will

Species: *Caprimulgus vociferous*

Popular and common variants/subspecies/other names: Nightjar, goatsucker

Geographic distribution: Whip-poor-wills are found in southeastern Canada, eastern United States, Mexico, and Central America.

Environment: These birds are found in woodland.

Physical description: The whip-poor-will has a large head for its size, a small bill, and a short neck. It measures approximately 9 inches long, with a wingspan of about 18 inches and a weight of almost

2 ounces. The plumage is speckled or mottled brown, black, and gray—ideal for camouflage on the ground in fallen leaves or on bark.

Interesting facts: The whip-poor-will is commonly heard but less often seen because of its superior camouflage. It is named onomato-poeically after its call, which is said to be loudest and most frequent at dusk. It is a nocturnally active bird. The whip-poor-will lays its eggs according to the lunar cycle so its chicks hatch approximately ten days before the full moon.

Myths, folklore, and cultural associations: One New England legend says the whip-poor-will can sense a soul departing and can capture it as it flees. If you hear a whip-poor-will after dark (some beliefs say at midnight), it is a sign that someone you know will die. Other versions of this piece of folklore say that if the whip-poor-will is heard calling near a house, an inhabitant of that house will soon die.

As the goatsucker, the whip-poor-will is thought to have drained milk from goats or other farmyard animals, but this is unfounded. The birds are more likely to be snapping up insects disturbed from the ground by the animals' steps.

A whip-poor-will seen in an orchard is said to be unlucky, and ill fortune will be visited on someone who sees two whip-poor-wills flying together. However, if you point at a whip-poor-will in flight, it will cease flying. Another piece of folklore says that if a whip-poor-will is mocked, your house will be destroyed in a fire. And yet another says that whatever you are doing when you hear the first whip-poor-will call of the year indicates how the rest of your year will unfold. The call of the whip-poor-will was a significant omen to an unmarried wom-an: if she heard its call once, she would not marry for at least twelve months; if it called twice, a wedding would be held; if it called three times, she would remain a spinster. The latter could be avoided if she immediately wished for matrimony upon hearing the first call, but only if she kept the wish secret.

Omens and divinatory meaning: The whip-poor-will's excellent camouflage means that it is usually identified by its sound alone. The whip-poor-will brings you the message that your voice and what you say are more important than how you present yourself visually.

The whip-poor-will is always in tune with lunar cycles. The moon is associated with feminine energy, cycles, intuition, psychic energy, emotions, receptivity, and similar issues. Take a look at the feminine energy in your life. Is it in proper balance with the more projective masculine energies? The whip-poor-will may be calling you to look deeper into yourself, to attune yourself to the mysteries associated with the moon and its qualities.

Associated energies: Voice over appearance, lunar energy

Associated seasons: Fall, winter

Element associations: Earth, air

Color associations: Brown, black, gray

Woodpecker

Name: Downy woodpecker

Species: *Picoides pubescens*

Popular and common variants/subspecies/other names: Hairy woodpecker, red-headed woodpecker, sapsucker, pileated woodpecker (note: the illustration depicts a pileated woodpecker)

Geographic distribution: Species of woodpecker are found all over the world except in Australia, New Zealand, and the polar regions. The downy woodpecker, one of the most widespread species, is found throughout Canada and most of the United States; the hairy woodpecker is found in the same North American regions as well as through Mexico and Central America.

Environment: Woodpeckers are partial to thickly forested areas, although some species live in treeless areas.

Physical description: A wide variety of size and plumage can be found among woodpeckers. The downy woodpecker is approximately 6 inches long, with a wingspan averaging 10 inches and a weight of just under an ounce. It has a white belly, black wings speckled with white, a black mask across the eyes, and a red crest on its head. The hairy woodpecker looks very similar to the downy woodpecker, only bigger.

Interesting facts: There are about 200 species in the Picidae family. The downy woodpecker has no call; instead, it is identified by the hard drumming sound it makes by hitting its bill against wood or sometimes even metal. This isn't a feeding action; rather, it is a separate movement that seems to substitute for a call or song. The downy woodpecker makes surprisingly little sound as it digs into wood to extract insects and grubs or to hollow out nesting cavities. A woodpecker's brain is packed tightly into its skull to protect it from the repeated rapid impact with hard surfaces. The woodpecker has a stiff tail that it can use as a prop or for extra support.

Myths, folklore, and cultural associations: It is no surprise that a lot of woodpecker folklore is directly tied to the characteristic drumming or hammering activity the bird engages in. The woodpecker was thought to summon rain, especially if pecking in an orchard. These birds were also thought to have a mystical ability to open places that were latched or shut, possibly due to the knocking nature of the pecking.

Mongolian legend says that Moses turned a servant into a woodpecker for stealing his food, and ever since that day the woodpecker has had to eat dry wood. A similar Scottish legend says that the woodpecker was once an old woman who refused to share her food with Jesus, and she now has to search for her food under the bark of trees.

Woodpecker feathers are said to be protection against being struck by lightning, and early American folklore says that if a woodpecker pecks at the corner of a house, death will come to one of the inhabitants.

Omens and divinatory meaning: If the woodpecker shows itself to you, it is a message that you have the key to something. The woodpecker tells you that you can, in fact, access what you thought or believed to be shut away or hidden from you.

The woodpecker also advises you to be hardheaded and focused; work hard and you will get results. Don't be swayed or turned away by what seems to be an impossible task. The woodpecker's stiff tail and well-packed brain also suggest that you should brace yourself for what may seem like an impenetrable challenge. But remember, you have the key that will allow you to pass.

The colors of the woodpecker—black, white, and red—are traditionally associated with the figure of the Triple Goddess (maiden, mother, crone). A woodpecker with these three colors can be passing you a message to examine your relationship with the feminine face of the Divine.

> **Associated energies:** Determination and commitment, stubbornness, Goddess energies, focus, safe passage
>
> **Associated seasons:** Summer, fall
>
> **Element associations:** Air, earth
>
> **Color associations:** Black, white, red

Wren

Name: House wren

Species: *Troglodytes aedon*

Popular and common variants/subspecies/other names: Winter wren, marsh wren, Eurasian wren

Geographic distribution: Wrens are found throughout Canada, the United States, Central America, and South America. The Eurasian wren is found in central Eurasia, with the densest population to the east and west, and Africa.

Environment: Wrens live in woodland, forest edges, grassland, agricultural areas, and residential areas.

Physical description: The house wren is a small brown bird, plumper than a sparrow, with pale speckles or bars on its short wings. It has a long beak and a longish tail. It measures approximately 5 inches long, with a wingspan of about 6 inches and a weight of half an ounce.

Interesting facts: Wren's eggs are very sensitive to temperature. If the eggs warm to above 106°F (41°C) for an hour, they will die; if the temperature drops below 65°F (18°C), the eggs may also be jeopardized. The house wren will fight larger birds for optimal nest boxes, crevices, or hollows. First-time male breeders will settle close to an older male in order to observe and pick up tricks regarding nesting.

Myths, folklore, and cultural associations: Much of the mythology associated with the wren comes from the Old World, although the wren as a species is more prevalent in the New World.

In England wrens were protected all year except on St. Stephen's Day, the day after Christmas, when they were hunted, trapped, then taken to visit each house in a village, and later killed solemnly. This practice appears to be the last remaining vestige of an obscure ritual, likely connected to the myth that a robin and a wren battle one another at the winter solstice, and the robin triumphs, killing the wren and bringing back the sun. (Presumably this would be reversed at the summer solstice, with the wren being the victor.)

The wren is said to be the king of birds. The birds held a competition to see who could fly highest, agreeing that whoever did would be crowned the king. The eagle flew the highest, but when it reached the apex of its flight the wren, who had hidden itself in the feathers on the eagle's back, peeped that it was actually higher, and thus the wren was crowned because it had technically reached a greater height than the eagle. (There is a similar myth about the thrush demonstrating cunning by stowing away on the eagle's back in order to be granted the most beautiful song of all; see Thrush.)

Folklore has Jenny Wren as the wife of Robin Redbreast, an interesting pairing considering the robin/wren battle of the winter solstice.

The wren is said to dive into the mouths of crocodiles to clean their teeth, and a wren's feathers were thought to be amulets against drowning. *Wren* was once one of the many bird-related euphemisms for a prostitute.

Omens and divinatory meaning: The wren is a clever, cocky bird. If it shows itself to you, it may be telling you to use your wits in standing up to someone or something bigger or stronger than you in order to accomplish your goal.

The wren's sensitivity to temperature may also be a message. Watch for extremes in your behavior; stay in your comfort zone. Keep everything in balance and don't go out on a limb for the time being. You operate best within a certain range of comfort, be that physical, mental, or emotional. Now is not the time to push yourself beyond your comfort level. Keep in mind that this message does not contradict the first point above; the two should work together in order to ensure that you operate at maximum efficiency for best success.

A younger wren's habit of settling close to an older one during its first season alone can be an important message too. Look to someone more experienced for ideas and tips about your situation or seek out a mentor.

Associated energies: Family, home, balance, strength, courage

Associated season: Summer

Element association: Air

Color associations: Brown, gray

Yellow Warbler

Species: *Dendroica petechial*

Popular and common variants/subspecies/other names: Yellowbird, yellowhammer, wild canary

Geographic distribution: Yellow warblers are found in northern Canada, Alaska, south through the United States, and Mexico, and winter in Central America and the northern tip of South America. Old World warblers are found mainly in Asia and Africa.

Environment: The yellow warbler prefers forests with water or wet areas nearby.

Physical description: The yellow warbler is a small songbird with bright yellow to greenish-yellow plumage. Males have rust stripes on the chest. On average, this bird measures 5 inches long, with a wingspan of 7 inches and a weight of about a third of an ounce.

Interesting facts: The warbler migrates at night, resting during the day. Apart from the bright yellow coloring, the yellow warbler is perhaps best known for its sweet song, a bright sequence of six to eight notes.

Myths, folklore, and cultural associations: Like some other unrelated birds who bear the same names, Old World warblers and New World warblers are not related, but the mythology and cultural associations transfer.

This bird's name suggests the sweetness of its voice and song. The term *warbler* is assigned to a singer who is particularly adept at vocal embellishment, although colloquially it is used to describe a singer in general. The Japanese bush-warbler is sometimes called "the poem-reading bird," associating it further with the arts.

A folk name for a yellow warbler is yellowhammer, although they do not hammer their beaks on wood the way a woodpecker does.

Omens and divinatory meaning: The warbler's primary message is to celebrate the joys in your life. Sing out; be cheerful; honor your bright colors; be proud of what you are and what you have achieved.

Warblers are, of course, associated with the voice. How is the health of your throat? Singing is also a form of creative expression. Are you fully expressing yourself, or are you marginalizing creative expression in favor of things such as work or intellectual pursuits? Engaging in creative activity has great value—not only does it exercise a different part of your brain but it relaxes and refreshes you as well. Having creative problem-solving skills at your disposal can help you in everyday life. The yellow warbler also encourages you to look for the beauty in life. Unlike other birds who have sweet voices but dull plumage, the warbler demonstrates beauty both aurally and visually.

Because the warbler uses nighttime for migratory travel and rests during the day, it suggests a reversal of usual patterns. If you're having trouble accomplishing certain tasks at a particular time of day, try scheduling them during a different hour.

Associated energies: Joy, celebration, creativity

Associated season: Summer

Element association: Air

Color associations: Yellow, gold

Resource List

Andrews, Ted. *Animal-Speak: The Spiritual & Magical Powers of Creatures Great & Small*. St. Paul, Minn.: Llewellyn Publications, 2000.

Carbone, G.G., and Mary Ruzicka. *Bird Signs: Guidance & Wisdom from Our Feathered Friends*. Novato, Calif.: New World Library, 2007.

Clements, James F. *The Clements Checklist of Birds of the World*, 6th ed. Ithaca, NY: Cornell University Press, 2007.

Cunningham, Scott. *Divination for Beginners: Reading the Past, Present & Future*. St. Paul, Minn.: Llewellyn Publications, 2003.

Daniels, Cora Linn, and C.M. Stevans, eds. *Encyclopaedia of Superstitions, Folklore, and the Occult Sciences of the World*, vols. 1–3. Honolulu: University Press of the Pacific, 2003.

Gibson, Graeme. *The Bedside Book of Birds: An Avian Miscellany*. London: Bloomsbury Publishing, 2005.

Holbrook, Florence. *The Book of Nature Myths*. www.gutenberg.org/ebooks/22420. Accessed 25 September 2018.

Martin, Laura C. *The Folklore of Birds*. Old Saybrook, Conn: Globe Pequot Press, 1993.

Matthews, John, ed. *The World Atlas of Divination*. Boston: Bulfinch Press, 1992.

Morrison, Lesley. *The Healing Wisdom of Birds: An Everyday Guide to Their Spiritual Songs & Symbolism*. Woodbury, Minn.: Llewellyn Publications, 2011.

National Audubon Society. *The National Audubon Society Field Guide to North American Birds, Eastern Region*. New York: Alfred A. Knopf, 1995.

———. *The National Audubon Society Field Guide to North American Birds, Western Region*. New York: Alfred A. Knopf, 1995.

Peterson, Roger Tory. *Peterson Field Guide to Birds of Eastern and Central North America*, 5th ed. Boston: Houghton Mifflin, 2002.

Thoreau, Henry David. *The Heart of Thoreau's Journals*. Odell Shepard, ed. Mineola, NY: Dover Publications, 1961.

Wansbury, Andrea. *Birds, Divine Messengers: Transform Your Life with Their Guidance and Wisdom*. Forres, Scotland: Findhorn Press, 2006.

Weidensaul, Scott. *The Birder's Miscellany: A Fascinating Collection of Facts, Figures, and Folklore from the World of Birds*. New York: Fireside Books, 1991.

Wells, Diana. *100 Birds and How They Got Their Names*. Chapel Hill, NC: Algonquin Books of Chapel Hill, 2002.

Websites

Cornell Lab of Ornithology: www.birds.cornell.edu

National Audubon Society: www.audubon.org/birds

Aesopica: Aesop's Fables in English, Latin, and Greek: www.mythfolklore.net/aesopica

Articles

"Much-maligned waxwing makes return trip to WWF," wwf.panda.org/?155221/much-maligned-waxwing-makes-return-trip-to-wwf

US/Metric Conversion Chart

LENGTH CONVERSIONS	
US LENGTH MEASURE	**METRIC EQUIVALENT**
¼ inch	0.6 centimeters
½ inch	1.2 centimeters
¾ inch	1.9 centimeters
1 inch	2.5 centimeters
1½ inches	3.8 centimeters
1 foot	0.3 meters
1 yard	0.9 meters
WEIGHT CONVERSIONS	
US WEIGHT MEASURE	**METRIC EQUIVALENT**
½ ounce	15 grams
1 ounce	30 grams
2 ounces	60 grams
3 ounces	85 grams
¼ pound (4 ounces)	115 grams
½ pound (8 ounces)	225 grams
¾ pound (12 ounces)	340 grams
1 pound (16 ounces)	454 grams

Index

About the Author

Arin Murphy-Hiscock is a third-degree Wiccan High Priestess in the Black Forest Clan and the author of the bestselling book *The Green Witch: Your Complete Guide to the Natural Magic of Herbs, Flowers, Essential Oils, and More*, among others. She has been active in the New Age community since 1995 and publishing books since 2005. She lives in Montreal, Canada, with her husband and two children.